I0473300

Alexandr KALININ

Igor OSETSIMSKIY

Alex AL-VATAR

THE FLOW OF CLIENTS

FROM

FACEBOOK AND

INSTAGRAM

How to make money with social media

A handbook for entrepreneurs and professionals

Text Copyright ©

[Alexandr KALININ,
Igor OSETSIMSKIY,
Alex AL-VATAR]

All rights reserved. No part of this guide may be reproduced in any form without permission in writing from the publisher except in the case of brief quotations embodied in critical articles or reviews.

Legal & Disclaimer

The information contained in this book and its contents is not designed to replace or take the place of any form of medical or professional advice; and is not meant to replace the need for independent medical, financial, legal or other professional advice or services, as may be required. The content and information in this book have been provided for educational and entertainment purposes only.

The content and information contained in this book have been compiled from sources deemed reliable, and it is accurate to the best of the Author's knowledge, information and belief. However, the Author cannot guarantee its accuracy and validity and cannot be held liable for any errors and/or omissions. Further, changes are periodically made to this book as and when needed. Where appropriate and/or necessary, you must consult a professional (including but not limited to your doctor, attorney, financial advisor or such other professional advisor) before using any of the suggested remedies, techniques, or information in this book.

Upon using the contents and information contained in this book, you agree to hold harmless the Author from and against any damages, costs, and expenses, including any legal fees potentially resulting from the application of any of the information provided by this book. This disclaimer applies to any loss, damages or injury caused by the use and application, whether directly or indirectly, of any advice or information presented, whether for breach of contract, tort, negligence, personal injury, criminal intent, or under any other cause of action.

You agree to accept all risks of using the information presented in this book.

You agree that by continuing to read this book, where appropriate and/or necessary, you shall consult a professional (including but not limited to your doctor, attorney, or financial advisor or such other advisor as needed) before using any of the suggested remedies, techniques, or information in this book.

The book immerses the reader in the world of Internet marketing and social networks and explains how to be good at modern technologies of business promotion and development. The book includes a lot of recommendations that will help make online advertising more effective. The proposed methods will contribute to the growth of sales and brand awareness without increasing the advertising budget. A huge number of experience-based strategies will bring any business to the next level and make your decision-making process more skilful. The authors tried to create a very useful book for people interested in social marketing. It is aimed to serve as a handbook for entrepreneurs who have decided to independently understand the concepts of social media marketing, as well as a source of ideas for specialists.

TABLE OF CONTENTS

The flow of clients from Facebook and Instagram

Learning has never been as popular as it is today. All the boundaries between possible and impossible got erased, as everyone aspires to take their part in this fast-paced development of technologies, methods and practices. Therefore, there are so many people willing to learn something new and on the other hand, there are so many people offering to teach. Unfortunately, there aren`t so many practitioners among these "teachers". Many of them simply retell the theory, thus reducing the value of the learning process.

Nevertheless, there are those who accumulate their experience and then wholeheartedly share it. For example, the authors of the "The Flow of Clients from Facebook and Instagram", Alexandr Kalinin, Igor Osetsimskiy and Alex Al-Vatar. Each of them has been an expert in his given field of activity. Each of them worked their way from endeavours' and mistakes and gained both the knowledge and the experience, which they are now offering to entrepreneurs and marketing experts. The authors have a huge number of successful projects because they know how to act properly under the present-day conditions in order to achieve prominent results. They have applied their knowledge in absolutely different businesses, where they hadn't estimated their results by the money earned, but by the experience gained and by the value of their actions for their clients.

The journey they had allowed the authors to unite all the knowledge and determine their personal formula of success, which they are sharing in the present book. The book is full of personal examples from their own business experience, as well as the stories of their clients. Such stories do not only teach but also serve as a source of inspiration.

Moreover, the book thoroughly explores different strategies of promotion in social networks, shares the secrets of successful advertising campaigns as well as the ins and outs of building a personal brand. In addition, the book covers all the topics taking into account all the hidden pitfalls and gives recommendations on how to act in specific situations.

This book stands out with its attention to the finest details and insights that nobody usually mentions, but which are extremely important in the creation of successful business on the Internet.

Introduction
Aleks AL-VATAR

Speaking to small business owners and professionals, we often recommend them to start setting up advertising on Facebook and Instagram without any assistance. Don`t be afraid to master this skill. It will be unprofitable to contact a marketer and pay for their services in the beginning, when you are only trying to attract customers via the web and have small budgets (30-100USD per month, for example) available, since you will have to pay the marketer approximately $200 more for setting up an advertising campaign and dealing with social networks. Instead, you could spend this money on training, consulting, and learning how to attract clients from social networks yourself. Later, when you see the result and understand how advertising works, how to create the content, manage your accounts and make publications, as well as how much money it brings you, then you will be able to delegate these tasks to a marketing professional if you would feel like you need their services.

Applying for the services of a marketing specialist does not mean it would guarantee an inflow of new clients from social networks. In most cases, marketers know how specialized tools and software work. They know the interface of the program and which buttons to click on to launch ads and spend money on showing your offer to potential customers. It is essential to recall that it's not enough to just be a professional marketer in order to attract clients from social networks because you also need to be an entrepreneur to some extent.

It often happens that for effective advertising on the Internet you need to create new products and services offered by your business. The marketologists will not do that for you, but the entrepreneur will do. That is why there are two paths you can choose from. The first one means that you shall study online marketing basics yourself. The second one lies in the fact that you should find a marketing professional with entrepreneurial experience who understands how the business works, and not just how the marketing services and tools work. But the time of such specialists and collaboration with them, of course, will cost much more.

At the same time, entrepreneurs, who own profitable businesses, may conclude that they would not be interested in learning marketing strategies and it would even not be profitable for them to plunge into social networks, because they have other goals. Such people believe that everyone has different skills, well horses for courses. Usually, these are the executive managers of large companies or founders who completely left operations management. And they are also right. But in this case, they need to choose a good marketing specialist to work with. This can be done during a conversation or an interview.

However, you can understand the competence of a marketing specialist only if you have some knowledge of at least about the possibilities of advertising on Facebook and Instagram and understand the criteria for making decisions in marketing. You will be able to ask proper questions in order to determine the marketologist's competence, only if you know what are experienced specialists paying attention to, how do they choose a promotion strategy, how do they create all the content and what tricks do they use to customize advertising.

In addition, there is a myth that any advertising on the Internet requires a lot of money to spend on it. On the one hand, yes, it is true. There are companies that spend thousands of dollars on their social media promotion. On the other hand, you can start with only 10-50 dollars. In some cases, this is enough to attract the first customers, sell a product or service, return the money spent on advertising, and continue your own promotion. Of course, everything depends on your business model, service and other factors.

With all that said, we have created this book. If you read it down to the last page, you will have a basic understanding of social media marketing. This will happen even if you don't understand anything in how Facebook and Instagram work, or you neither have any experience, nor own website.

In this manual, we have shared our experience obtained while working on hundreds of business projects. The knowledge you will get will help you attract customers from Facebook and Instagram, save money on advertising, create better content, find qualified employees and much more.

When we were writing this book, we wanted to create some criteria for you to make it easier to take effective marketing decisions. That is why we have paid so much attention to some questions through the pages of this book and shared many illustrative examples from our own experience, just to help you understand how Facebook and

Instagram ads work and how to create a stream of clients from social networks.

So just relax and trust us. If you encounter some things that might not be clear to you, you should not put the book away for later. Do not immediately implement everything that is written in the book. Just read it. Along with reading, or after finishing the book you will start noticing that when working with social networks, you are paying attention to the details that you have not been taking into consideration before. You will understand the possibilities of advertising, which you couldn't even imagine before. This book will change your beliefs about the world of Facebook and Instagram.

We wish you the best of luck!

Have fun reading!

Chapter 1: PROMOTION STRATEGIES IN DIFFERENT NICHE MARKETS
Alexandr Kalinin

I usually highlight three promotion strategies.

There is a huge number of tools for promotion in social networks. We will definitely reveal all of them throughout this book. However, it is necessary to choose a correct promotion strategy to make all these tools work properly for you.

Everyone knows that in order to build a house or even to make a chair, you need a lot of different tools. And each tool has its own purpose.

Therefore, it is vital to choose the right strategy and don't try to batter down a nail using a screwdriver, as it's simply unproductive and inefficient.

There are three main promotion strategies on Facebook and Instagram:

- Direct sales of goods,
- Sales by means of 'lead-magnet' strategy,
- Sales through utility, which is creating an audience on Facebook and Instagram.

And now let's analyze each of these strategies, starting with direct sales of goods.

Direct sales of goods

This strategy means the sale of goods or services directly to people.

For example, there are a lot of sales representatives who break into offices and offer to buy some goods. As a rule, they offer books, protective films and phone covers, some very profitable memberships, etc. I even bought such membership at a bowling club once, although I am not inclined to make quick purchasing decisions.

But I purchased it, I succumbed to this temptation, because the offer was limited, and it was an opportunity to save money.

On social networks, `direct sale of goods` looks like this:

- you write an advertising text or record a video with an offer to purchase your goods or services;
- you use it for your advertising campaign;
- people see your offer and buy your products or services.

Should you use this strategy? Yes. Of course, you should have this strategy in your arsenal, because there are some people who will really immediately purchase your product or service. This strategy might be used for those goods, sale of which goes through emotional contacts. These can be any inexpensive goods that cost less than 25 dollars.

Nevertheless, do not use this strategy for all your products. Why?

It is easy to explain. How many of you got up this morning with the thought that you really need to buy something on Facebook or on Instagram? Most likely, no one. Most often, you hit the social media platforms to communicate with your friends and acquaintances, tell about yourself or learn something new.

Choosing the strategy of `direct sales of goods`, you will work with people who are already willing to purchase a product or service. But this is a minority.

This strategy reminds me of my job in a hardware company. I worked in a retail store where I was selling personal computers and components to ordinary people. People often came to the store to get some advice, for example: which PC to opt for and, of course, to buy something too.

After a year of work in this retail store, I was promoted to the corporate department. But it only looked like a`promotion`, as my responsibilities didn't change, I still had to sell various hardware and equipment, but now - to companies.

If the people, coming to my retail store, were already interested in buying certain component parts, the number of companies willing to buy or update their equipment was insignificant, as, in addition, most of them weren't even looking for that equipment.

And I had to call the offices of these companies and search for the people responsible for the purchase of equipment to offer my goods. I was making about 100 calls per day, 99 of which were ending in disappointment. People were simply flipping me off. That makes sense because people didn`t know ANYTHING about me, or about my company, or about the products I was offering.

You will have the same statistics if you will use just the strategy of `direct sales of goods`. By the way, these are the normal stats for any online store, when only 1 person out of 100 makes an order.

But I got some good experience, which formed the basis of my business promotion strategy on social networks.

At first, I need to build a trusting relationship and only then sell something.

Nowadays, our world is overfilled with advertising. Ads are everywhere, on every corner of every street. We became so accustomed to this that sometimes we don't even pay attention to advertisements. If you sell a product directly through your advertisement, there is a high probability that you will not have any major success with it. People can be really weird, they like to buy things, but don't like when somebody tries to sell them something.

You know it is like walking down the street and meet a seller of mobile phones with insane discounts. It is very suspicious. And even if it's a real phone, you will not buy it. You never know: maybe this phone is stolen, defective, or something else.

The same happens with your advertising. Imagine your client who is sitting in a cafe, drinking delicious coffee with a chocolate croissant and lazily scrolling through their feed on Facebook or Instagram. And suddenly, he is offered to buy a product, be it a training course, underwear or something else. How do you think, will he buy it?

Everyone sells their products in the same way and, of course, advertising begins to annoy people. This is understandable. There are just too many sellers who use the same methods, making them totally inefficient.

Therefore, it makes no sense to sell your products directly and immediately. Why should your target audience hear you amid all this advertising noise? Why should they buy exactly your product? What is your uniqueness: is it the attractive price or packaging, or maybe warrantees? Or do you offer more for less?

Yes, I understand that your product is the best. I understand that you care about your customers, but people on the social networks do not know this, and for them, all the sellers are as identical as two peas. In order to become attractive for your audience, it is vital for you to become useful to your audience and not just another seller of another product. You will gain more trust when you start helping people, and then you will break stereotypes because you will not be trying to sell your product all the time. Instead of this, try to build a community around you that will be with you for many years.

That is why, by choosing the strategy of `direct sales of goods `, you are depriving your business of a huge audience you could interact with in a different way.

The second strategy is selling through lead magnets

A lead magnet is a free product that brings customers in exchange for valuable information about themselves, for example, their contact details (name, e-mail, phone number, link to the social network).

Consultation, mini-book, video lessons, test drive, master class, private webinar, open day, free course, pdf document, commercial offer, discount coupon or checklist - any of these can serve as a lead magnet.

One of the most frequent examples of a lead magnet is a consultation. It allows you to communicate with a client, show your skills, answer all the troubling questions, deal with objections and thereby close the deal. A few years ago, l worked with a client whose company was producing customized kitchen furniture, priced around $3000–5000.

He wanted to launch an advertising campaign to promote the furniture he was producing on Facebook and Instagram. However, it is quite difficult to sell such a product on Facebook, because it`s necessary to take measurements, choose materials and colour to buy the kitchen furniture. Therefore, there was no call for purchase in the promotional offer, and it looked like this: `Order a free measurement and

get the 3D model of your dream kitchen furniture as a gift`
and `Get a free counselling with a specialist with a personal
on-site measurement`.

I did the same with a real estate agency, where we
were not offering the potential customers to buy an
apartment immediately but made the next simple checklist:
`10 ways to buy an apartment profitably` and offered to
download it for free. I can assure you no one will refuse to
receive such a list of actions and save money on the
purchase.

For an educational project of a nutritionist, who
offered weight-loss courses, we came up with such a lead
magnet:` Get three video lessons about losing weight easily
without dieting and exhausting workouts in the gym`.

That was the way we received considerable lists of
people who were really interested in the given subject and
later we used these lists to offer them more expensive
products or services.

The third strategy is selling through utility

The third strategy involves gathering audiences around you. The task of this strategy is to show that you are the best expert in your field and you can be trusted and thus gather a loyal audience.

I'm sure you saw people on Instagram who have a lot of subscribers. And each new post they publish receives a huge number of likes and comments. When you engage subscribers in your business and your personal lives, then the audience becomes very loyal to you or your company.

This is exactly the strategy that you need to strive because it will bring you much more sales and increase the company's revenues and make the jungle telegraph work effectively.

For most businesses, the jungle telegraph is the main source of customer acquisition. I am sure that you have the same experience. All the most loyal customers come upon the recommendations.

These are the people who do not need to be persuaded for too long, they know enough about you and are ready to make a purchase. For example, in my business, 80% of customers are people who came upon the recommendations of old customers.

Do more than you agreed with your client or partner. Share your useful information with other people. After all, your goal is to `exceed the expectations and give people usefulness even before they get to know you`.

That is what I did at the beginning of my business when I was just learning about online advertising. I provided free options to people and offered to create advertisements for their business. Besides the ads, I conducted a detailed analysis of their websites and created a large list of useful changes to improve their effectivity and attractivity.

Although we did not agree on this, it was only my initiative. And, you know, in some cases, I even made websites for free for customers to make my ads be effective.

It allowed me to turn off all the ads for a year since I received a huge number of customers thanks to the jungle telegraph. Everything that you do in your business, you must do for your customers. Be useful to people and you will be rewarded. It is guaranteed. But I must warn you that there is one pitfall, which once really spoiled my nerves.

Your option is useful to people ONLY if they have ever interacted with you at least once. In other cases, they won't be interested in your service.

So it was with me when I offered my services for setting up advertising. I wrote a cool advertising text about my free consultations on promoting online business and told about all my merits. I started advertising and in 2 days I received more than 20 applications, which cost me only $ 20, and started to call up with the people who left them.

Well, it was a big surprise for me. When I started to call, people answered that they did not remember their requests and asked to call back later. They found an excuse to postpone the option. I realized that I was doing something wrong! I realized that I am a regular seller for them, they have neither trust nor desire to buy my services.

Then I decided to take a different approach. I recorded a series of useful video clips and shared useful information on how to start advertising, to what everyone should pay attention to and how to engage with the audience and much more.

And only after people watched my videos, I offered them a note on my option. People were waiting for my option; everyone came on time and left rave reviews after the conversation.

`Useful content` is a series of useful videos or posts that analyses the needs of your target audience. Its purpose is to generate interest and create a desire to solve the affected problem, as well as introduce potential customers to you and grow their confidence. For these purposes, you can use articles and videos.

Similarly, I acted with the client who made customized kitchen furniture. His series of useful content was aimed at showing what problems may arise when ordering a low-quality cabinet or kitchen furniture. The articles were called 10 cabinet selection rules or 7 mistakes when choosing kitchen furniture, etc.

We made videos with the real estate agency, where we were sharing different life-hacks to buy an apartment and what to pay attention to when choosing it or about owner's mistakes when selling an apartment. We also spoke about where an owner can find buyers for the apartment. Later, we did the same for the client who was helping people lose weight. We asked different important questions such as `How does the way of cooking affect the food price?` `Is it easy and simple to introduce healthy and tasty food in your routine? `10 principles of right nutrition in the modern world`.

I hope you understood the core of the subject. In each article, we raise all the problems that potential customers will have to face. This content is very useful for them, and we, as specialists, get more trust. This `useful content` transforms your `cold audience` into a `warm` one.

Everything that I will discuss in this book, will be accompanied with examples because it will be easier to understand for the owners of almost any business.

A task for you. Write out 10 problems your clients might be facing and try to explain how to resolve them in your own articles or videos. Pay attention to this important detail. Believe me, this is the content that we most often used for advertising purposes. I hope you have already begun to do this task.

What else does the third strategy include? This is a community development on Facebook and Instagram, where you do not only sell products but also share useful materials, share your stories, stories of your clients and employees, train your clients. We will talk more about this strategy in the next chapters of our book.

Nowadays, people are buying from people. There is a person behind each company, so a personal brand has great importance. It is easier and more pleasant for people to buy from an honest person, and if this person is also an expert in their business, then sales become a matter of technology.

We will explain how to choose a strategy when starting the promotion on Facebook and Instagram in the next chapter, as well as what criteria of decision-making exist when choosing a particular strategy.

What would be the main decision-making criteria

when choosing a strategy for your ads on Facebook

and Instagram?

In the latter chapter, we covered all the strategies. I'm sure you already have an understanding of what strategy to choose. But let us determine exactly which strategy is worth to choose and why.

Remember how you chose your last phone. You may have seen it anywhere, and you wanted `the same`. This is especially true when it comes to ladies who often want the same `as my friend Jane has`.

So, you came to a store (or an online store). There are so many mobile phones! But you came to get the one you have seen. OK, it is very beautiful, and in 10 minutes it can be yours.

But at the same time, you want a `pink` one with the local memory of at least 64 GB and a screen of at least 4 inches.

These criteria are very important to you. And if this beautiful phone does not meet any of the criteria that are important for you, of course, you begin to doubt and look for similar options.

So, are there any basic criteria by which we understand this phone is the best for us?

Similarly, it happens with the criteria for promotion on Facebook and Instagram, which help us to decide what strategy to use to create an advertising campaign.

There are four main criteria:
- the price of the product or service;
- the sale`s time cycle;
- the number of stages of the bargain;
- warm and cold audiences.

The criterion of the value of the products, goods, services

Do you remember your most expensive purchase? Was it a house, a car, a trip, training? It doesn't matter which one you'll pick. The most expensive purchase recalled? Fine! How much information have you had on hand about it before buying? That's right, a lot of information! You knew everything about all the guarantees, found people who have already used something you were going to buy, and got their feedback, learned all the information about the seller (Can you trust them? How many years of experience they have? Are there any negative reviews?).

You were doing all this because you were going to pay a lot of money, and it was important to be sure that everything will be fine. Now, remember how you bought the latest T-shirt or shorts in the store. Probably, you had a thought: `Oh, what a cool T-shirt, I just need one. I'll take even 2 because of the second discount`.

It is also easy to buy baby products, especially when you go shopping with children. After all, children want everything they see. All these are emotional purchases: `I want`, `Wow`, `Mom buy me this robot, I have never had such a thing`. When it isn`t expensive, you can easily decide. It turns out that the higher the cost of your product, service or training is, the more information, guarantees, evidence people need to make a purchase decision.

Well, in case you offer cheap products and services up to $25, then you can safely try to sell them directly. People buy such goods emotionally. A lot of people can easily buy them, and not spend a lot of time to decide to buy it or not. Guided by such a criterion as `price`, you can understand which strategy you should choose: either opt for direct sales or find a lead magnet with which you can attract potential customers.

The criterion of the sale`s time cycle

Recently, I repaired my apartment and understood these criteria. The remodelling in the apartment has just begun. The worker was only doing the floor and I had to choose the interior doors. In fact, a month before the purchase, I went to choose the doors. I was in all the shops in the city and then reviewed all the sites on the Internet. I found out the prices, quality, re-read several articles on how to choose the right interior doors.

All my training lasted more than 30 days. And only after that, I made a purchase decision.

In this case, we are guided by two criteria: the sale`s time cycle and the number of stages of the bargain. If your potential client has to spend a lot of time on making a purchase decision (as I did when choosing my interior doors), then selling directly is definitely not for you.

I have a client who manufactures cabinets and kitchen furniture, and it takes from 2 to 6 months for his clients to make a decision about buying a set of kitchen furniture. That`s why from the moment when a potential client approached you until the moment when he ordered a cupboard, a sufficiently long period of time can pass and the seller's task, in this case, is to interact with the client all this time.

Therefore, the `utilities` strategy works perfectly when you create a community, share your expert opinions and interact with the client until the moment of purchase. So, when they decide to buy, they will most likely do it with you.

The criterion of the number of bargain's stages

This is like going to the doctor. The doctor will not be able to treat a disease if he does not examine and does not require certain tests. Later, he will be able to prescribe proper treatment for you.

There are a number of businesses, primarily offering services, where you cannot make a sale without a personal meeting.

In my business, it exactly means that without a prior meeting with a client, without details about their business, I cannot offer him proper service for promotion on the Internet. I need to know what methods were already used, what results they gave and some information about the website. As you understand, there are a lot of questions. As a rule, this criterion applies to all services. And if this happens in your business as well, then the second strategy is ideal for you. Invite people for a personal meeting, calculate the price and draw up a commercial proposal, etc.

The criterion of warm and cold audiences

I will introduce a new concept: the warmth of the audience. What does it mean? For convenience, we will divide the audience into two types: cold and warm. Cold audiences include some people who know nothing about you, have never come across you and have not seen you either online or personally. Warm audiences include some people who are already your customers or subscribers or have somehow already communicated with your materials on the Internet. For example, they watched videos, commented on advertising posts or interacted with your business in any way.

The warm audience can be divided into two types:
your customer base
people who are not yet your customers.

The first category of people can be offered any additional goods or services. People from the second category can be offered a lead magnet or product directly. Most likely, you have such an audience, and there are many of them. In this case, Facebook offers a huge amount of tools to interact with a warm audience. In the chapter, we will learn more about the possibilities of targeted advertising.

Once upon a time, a girl named Alexandra came to me. She was the lead trainer in the `School of Eloquence`, where at that time more than 1000 people had already been trained. By the way, I also took this course, and it was a very rewarding experience that gave me a good start for public speaking. So, the purpose of the appeal was to help in gathering a group of people for the course, which was about to start very soon. And then a question was which promotion strategy to choose? Our goal was to assemble a group and do it quite quickly, because of the nearby beginning of the course.

During the work of the School of Eloquence more than 3000 people subscribed to its page on Facebook, 1000 people on the Youtube channel and on Instagram, as well as a base of phone numbers of customers who took the courses was collected.

These are all the people who have been interested in the topic of public speaking. So, we gathered the entire audience of subscribers on Facebook and Instagram, as well as people who were going to join the course, but did change their mind. They started advertising for these people with a proposal to sign up for a new course, which starts in 10 days.

Thus, in 10 days we received more than 70 applications from potential customers with the advertising budget of 150 dollars. The funds invested in advertising paid off tenfold.

Later, we will analyze various strategies for different niches in your business. Then, you will only have to decide for yourself which one is the best and which one you should start with.

Some features of the promotion of simple services in different social networks

By simple services, we mean low-cost services, making a decision to purchase which does not take a lot of time. It can be beauty salon services such as manicure, haircut, beautician services, depilation, as well as the services of a psychologist, a lawyer, a plumber, a photographer.

Let's look at the strategy for promoting such services. As you already know, there are three main strategies: direct sales, using lead magnets and using utile information to create an audience on Facebook and Instagram.

All three strategies are ideal for promoting your simple services. All you need is to post on your Facebook or Instagram page and invite people to come to you. This can also be done on the business page on Facebook and through advertising. We will analyze how to do this in the next chapter.

The strategy of direct sales means that you are directly offering people to buy your services. But here it is worth considering a few pitfalls.

I had the experience of promoting a beauty salon. The salon offered to purchase a package of five basic services. All of them were simple, cheap and necessary for the target audience. During the month of operation, we attracted more than 120 applications from potential customers for these services. The girls were calling, booking an appointment, but did not reach the salon, or they came only for the first procedure and did not agree to try the rest.

In this case, I recommended making an online payment option for the services. As soon as the client decided to sign up for services, they were offered to immediately pay for the first procedure or to arrange 5 procedures with a discount, which should be completed. So you will get rid of the problem when customers sign up and do not come or come only to the first procedure. Since everyone loves a discount, there will be a lot more records and returns.

The `utility ` strategy is ideal for simple services. It will help you create a large community of loyal customers who will recommend you to others and regularly come on their own too.

The `utility` strategy includes the promotion of a business page on Facebook and Instagram. All we need is to start regularly sharing useful information on your subject or niche. The keyword here is `regularly`. If this is done once a month, then nothing will happen.

It's like a workout. When you attend the gym three times a week, after a month you will see an amazing result. But if you did a workout once a month, it is unlikely that something would change in your life. Believe me, regularity is the tool that will make you successful in any field that you would promote. Therefore, regular content on Facebook will make you well-known, recognizable, help to close many customer objections and establish a trusting relationship with you. All you need is to just start sharing useful, interesting information with people. What you should write on Facebook and Instagram, we will examine in the following chapters.

Some features of the promotion of complex services

We have already said that there are services that we cannot sell without consultation or a preliminary meeting.

All the 'complex services' include furniture manufacturing, apartment remodelling, real estate sales, website development, advertising settings, design services, and construction. It is almost impossible to sell such services without prior consultation, measurement, discussion, budgeting, and commercial offer. That is why for complex services the strategy of direct selling is excluded.

Of course, you can really launch an advertisement and directly offer people to buy cabinetry, cupboard or a wardrobe. However, it is less probable that people will make such a decision quickly. And even if people, having seen your advertisement, think about the fact that it's time to change their kitchen unit, by the time of the decision they will hardly remember you.

Therefore, all the complex services are promoted only by the 'utility ' strategy. And your 'lead magnet' is launched into advertising. What you can offer to show your expertise and make somebody want to cooperate with you (consultation, measurement, etc.).

As you already know, all complex services have one feature - a long term to make a purchasing decision, so your main goal is to be visible to the client until the moment they decide to buy it. First of all, the client should remember you. Prove to the client that you are a reliable company, tell about those who are already working with you, show your backstage, show your finished product. All you need is to share useful information. It should be timely and constantly visible. And regular content does an excellent job with these goals.

Write out the top 20 questions that your customers regularly ask. As a rule, these questions concern their awarenesses, their doubts. And then start sharing your answers to these questions on Instagram and Facebook in such ways:

- a live stream where you raise these issues;
- write articles;
- make stories;
- offer promotions;
- tell your story, some stories of your employees and your clients;
- publish the results of your work in the "before-after" format;
- review your upcoming events and products;

- create questionnaires and manuals;
- give advice;
- train your customers.

Some features of the sale of expensive goods on Facebook and Instagram

Expensive goods include jewellery, gadgets, branded clothing and so on. If you remember how you usually buy expensive goods, you will immediately receive many answers to questions about how to sell them on social networks.

Expensive goods are sometimes sold directly, where the clients are immediately offered to be taken to a site to place an order. But as a rule, it is not as effective as you think. After all, most people do not buy immediately.

I had a very interesting experience in selling expensive goods directly. These were artificial Christmas trees, costing from $300 to $1000. Frankly speaking, it is not the cheapest accessory to buy.

These Christmas trees had to be sold in November and December. Only two months, when it is actually possible to do it.

We started the promotion at the end of November, and no matter what we did, we had no sales in November. Only in the middle of December, they started receiving calls from people interested in the goods. And even more, we began getting comments on social networks under our advertisements.

People weren't very happy to see the advertising of our trees, which cost about $800. Can you imagine what kind of comments we received? `Can this tree prepare me dinner and go to the grocery store without me? ` or "Can this tree can clean the house and walk the dog, and so on."

Only at the end of the year, we were able to sell several trees and return the money invested in advertising. The direct sale strategy wasn`t effective and we received no income. I'm still not sure that this product can be sold on social networks. Much more efficient was the contextual advertising on Google, where people were already looking for similar products and did not need to be persuaded. It was through such advertising that we sold all the other artificial Christmas trees in the batch. But at this stage, think about how people are looking for your goods or service. It may also be the most effective option for you to start with the contextual advertising on Google. The ideal strategy for expensive products is an attraction strategy. People will easily buy if they know who are you and will trust you. Work on it.

Some peculiarities of selling low-cost goods on social networks

These are the inexpensive goods, costing up to $30, for example, any children's toys, Chinese goods, low-cost clothing, shoes, etc. It is easy to deal with them, as we sell them directly on Facebook. I had a client who was selling cheap jewellery for girls. These were bracelets, charms, rings. He brought them from China in bulk. The task was to sell them. The product was beautiful and very cheap, so we wanted to show it to as many girls as possible.

In this case, there is no difference in what kind of advertising to run. First, we launched advertising on Google, which brought us around 200 orders per month. And then we moved the ads on Facebook and Instagram, wherein the very first month we received more than 150 sales at the lowest price.

With these products, you have almost no restrictions. The most important thing is to make sure the largest target audience sees your offer. Therefore, any advertising will be suitable, be it contextual, on Google, targeted advertising on Facebook and Instagram, advertising on Youtube and advertising from bloggers. And, of course, the strategy of attraction will bring you great benefits. Especially when selling some cheap goods or services. Share tips, usefulness and you will sell more. Gather a community around you.

Some peculiarities of selling training, courses, training

In the spring of 2018, I received a very interesting experience in organizing master classes in 11 cities across Ukraine. In each city, we held one master class. The number of participants varied from 70 to 200 people.

We gathered all the people for the events solely through advertising on Facebook and Instagram. Of course, I had many projects with gathering people for training before. We promoted conferences, workshops, training, all kinds of courses. I tried different promotion options, but not all were as effective as I would have liked. Therefore, I made several important rules from my experience.

Firstly, it is important to regularly communicate with subscribers and add them to the database. The subscriber base is very easy to form when you share useful materials, as well as use a lead magnet (when you offer people to download something free in exchange for their contact information).

Secondly, it is difficult to offer expensive training directly to a cold audience. For this purpose, the launch of advertising with a lead magnet is more suitable. While selling this training, you can try your warm audience. This distribution will be the most cost-effective in terms of advertising costs.

Thirdly, cheap live workshops are a very cool event, which is not difficult to gather people for. However, it is that strategy through which the expensive training is sold very well. The "utility strategy" is an ideal option for selling educational products.

Practical task

- Determine your strategy. It is better to choose several.
- Write down the criteria by which you can decide that this strategy is right for you.
- Write 5 options of what you can use as a lead magnet.
- Write down the 10 problems/desires/ questions your clients usually have when they contact you. And think about how you could help your audience. You can write articles, record a video, hold a live stream.

In the next chapter, we will talk about how to create content, what to publish, where to get ideas for publications, how to correctly alternate useful content and marketing, as well as how to create the content for the next 5–10 years.

CHAPTER 2

CONTENT FOR SOCIAL MEDIA

Alex Al-Vatar

No content — no online sales.

During our workshops held in various Ukrainian cities, I always bring up the same question to the audience: «Are there any entrepreneurs and specialists who want to have great sales?», and you know, almost everyone rises up their hands!

In this book, as well as during our events or training, we discuss different tools for attracting clients. At the same time, I believe the content is the most important tool, but, as a rule, they don't talk about it.

Online sales cannot exist without some quality content.

Let's assume that you want to sell a service on the Internet. Selling the product you can feel it, touch it. And the service? It is a process. How do you show it? It is interesting, isn`t it? The customer wants to see what he pays for before buying. If you do not have some photos and videos demonstrating the product, or texts describing the benefits and characteristics of the product, the client wouldn`t understand what they pay for. So, you can only show the result. For example, it is a new type of haircut, so just show it to your client, using before and after photos. Everybody wants to see what they pay for, and if they see, it brings more trust.

For instance, you can tell me that you can explain to the client what you are selling just through a simple phone conversation, and it isn`t necessary to create special content for goods and services.

Well, you might be right, partially. There are certain areas of activity where the sale takes place through a personal meeting. Usually, these are some very expensive goods or complex services, which are practically impossible to sell without personal contact with the client and coordination of details. However, the more important is the role of content in this situation.

The fact is, in order to strike a mega deal you should have clients' trust. People want to know about your experience and expertise before they contact you.

Let us say, you personally message people on social networks and offer your services. Set out the prices and send the invoice for payment. But who will pay money if your social media pages aren`t credible? If you don`t have professional photos and videos, you don`t share any stories about your life and business development, about the team, office, qualifications and so on.

Here is an interesting story about credibility on social networks. I was about to start my latest advertising on Facebook, this time it would be promoting my own book «The Endless Flow of Ideas on How to Create Content for Business».

The idea is as follows. Watching the advertising, people see my video, where I am holding a book in my hands and talking about why it should be purchased. Next to the video is the advertising text and a link to message me so that people can contact me through my business page. After the client clicks on this link, they will automatically receive a message to the messenger agent with a link to my site where they can learn more about the book, order it and pay.

Thus, the advertising campaign is launched. I received the first notification that an order has been received. I call back by the phone number that the customer indicated. The dialogue goes as follows:

- Good afternoon. You left a request on the site to buy our new book. I see the application yet there is no payment. Do you have any questions?

- Yes, send it, I will pay on delivery.

- Actually, we usually send books after the payment is done.

- Well, I don't know you. I had cases when I paid money, but I didn`t receive my goods.

- I'm not going to betray you, it is just that before sending the book, I usually leave an autograph for everyone and I just want to know for sure that you will pick up the shipment.

- I understand, but I don't know you personally. Why should I trust you?

- Well, I can send a link of my personal Facebook page to this number, add me as a friend, look I`m a real person, and I can be trusted.

The customer started laughing. He did not expect such an answer. Later, he wrote to me on Facebook and said that he liked my approach very much, and the book really fascinated him. He paid for the book, and I sent my book.

A few days later this person was in my city, offered to meet up and even invited me to visit his city. So, social networks bring people together, and with proper management of your pages, they will be the cause of great confidence in you.

I think you already understand that without content on the Internet there will be no sales. Therefore, the first thing you need to do at the beginning of your business on Facebook and Instagram is to provide content for the pages.

The appeal of personal pages

In our experience, a personal page sells better than a business page. A lot of people for some reason think that it is necessary to separate personal and business pages and run two accounts. I don`t do that and I don`t recommend it to you, only if you lead a dual life.

So, what should you have on your page to look credible? The next things:

profile picture

profile cover

contacts

personal information

postings

photo albums

videos

All this is necessary in order for your page to be credible so that people on the Internet can see you, read about you, find out contacts and connect with you. Don`t be afraid to create your personal page for selling. It is good for people to look at your profile and see photos related to work and personal life, read your helpful publications about services and stories about relationships. Your profession or business is a great part of your life.

For me, for example, my work is always a priority, and I completely plunge into it. If earlier I used social networks to communicate with friends, now I mostly communicate on social networks with my clients. Every day I receive dozens, sometimes hundreds of messages and all they come mainly from potential customers.

Start using your Facebook and Instagram page as a tool to make money and attract customers. You can talk to your friends by phone or even better - meet and have a good time talking live.

The appeal of business pages

If you want to run ads on Facebook, you need to know that you can only do this on the business page. If you still don't have it, create one.

For your Facebook business page, you need:
user-friendly page name

It is very important to immediately name the business page.

profile picture

If you have a store or a brand of goods, add a logo to your avatar. If you are a specialist, working for yourself and providing services, upload your profile photo of high quality. The photo should show your face.

profile cover

A high-quality photo with your products or your professional photo at work will be perfect for it. The cover should convey the energy field of your activity. Think about a photo that will best show people your business.

Your contacts

Be sure to include phone numbers, store addresses, email, a link to the site and other social networks. Anyone should be able to contact you.

Photo albums

You should have all the archives. Find photos of your employees, offices, photos from events where you participated. Create several photo albums and upload all the photos that you have in the high quality and which are related to your work. There might be even 100-500 photos. The more photos — the more trust. Do not upload images that are downloaded from the Internet. If there are any, it is better to remove them.

Videos

Again, the materials should be yours, copyrighted. Get video calls from your customers. Video reports from events in which you participated or organized. Perhaps you have useful video tutorials that you created for your YouTube channel or for customers.

News Feeds

To get started and start advertising it is enough to write a few useful and interesting articles about your activity and publish them. So, if a potential client enters your page, they will see that there are several publications, and will be able to know more about your business.

In general, this is enough for your page to look credible.

Some people think that in order to start advertising on Facebook and Instagram, you need to collect subscribers for years, create many publications and only after that you can start advertising. This is far from being the truth…

To start attracting customers with advertising, it is enough to just competently shape up your business page. The fact is that many of those who will see your ads may not look at your page at all. They will see your video or advertising text with a picture in the news feed, go to the site or leave their phone number so that you can contact them.

Nevertheless, it is necessary to launch a business page before setting up advertising to establish credibility.

In the spring of 2018, we planned our first joint tour with Igor Osetsimskiy and Alexandr Kalinin with a workshop for entrepreneurs and specialists around Ukraine. We planed to visit 10 cities and hold 12 workshops. In each city, we gathered from 100 to 200 people. And what do you think? Did we have a popular business page at that time? Not at all! We created it 2 weeks before we started running the ads. We had a lot of content that we uploaded onto the page, and so we tackled the issue of credibility. However, there were some people who said that we were not real, that we wouldn`t come. Hundreds of our photos from other workshops, professional photos in the studio, dozens of video reviews by our clients were published on the page, but still, there were those who didn`t believe us. So don`t worry if you run into lack of trust on the Internet, it simply means that you need to publish more photos, videos, and articles about yourself and your business.

Same happens to our clients. In 2017, a young woman, Catherine, contacted us. She was developing her own brand of women's clothing, and at that time she was using Instagram to sell her clothing lines, but she didn't work on Facebook and didn't attract customers. We met in a cafe and right during the meeting, using her smartphone we created a business page and a store on Facebook. We loaded her brand logo as the profile photo and the photo of her dress on the page cover. Later, our manager created a catalogue of products, uploaded photos and wrote texts for each item. We set up advertising, and in one month and around $100 spent on advertising, we received 24 orders for women's dresses and 11 sales with an average check of $ 50.

In other words, if you want to receive clients from all the corners of the country and advertise all over the nation, all you have to do is upload quality content on your page and set up advertising on Facebook and Instagram.

We will discuss how to set up advertising in the next chapter. You will learn about the possibilities that you do not use, as well as about the tricks and algorithms of your Facebook advertising office for setting up a successful advertising campaign.

I will tell more about this later. Now, you will learn what to publish on social networks to attract customers.

What to publish?

Your pages should be a reflection of your life. People surf the web and see your page. They don`t know you personally. They don`t know who you are, what you do, what hobbies you have. Your page on social networks and your publications is a great way to make acquaintances on the Internet, even when you are sleeping.

Just imagine, you spent 10 minutes and made a publication in the news feed to tell your story. And over the next few days, hundreds, maybe even thousands of people will read this story.

How much time would it take for you to tell this story to 1000 different people? That's awesome, isn't it?

And so, I have a set of criteria that helps me understand exactly what publications need to be present on the Internet. If I notice that in real life I am telling the same story several times to different people, for me, it is a signal that this story should be written down and published on social networks. If I want this story to be read by as many people as possible, then it is easier for me to spend 10 minutes and publish it on Facebook and Instagram than to tell it in person to everyone.

This can be related to your personal life as well as your work. For example, you noticed that before customers agree to purchase your product or service, you constantly tell them the same story about yourself or about your experience. This story can help potential customers make a purchase decision, and it makes you an expert. I am sure you will remember all the information you've been usually telling your customers before buying. All this can be published as content on the Internet.

So, what do you need to publish on Facebook and Instagram? How do you correctly publish your posts? Here are some types of content that I recommend to publish on a constant basis absolutely for all business projects:

- ✓ news and stories
- ✓ useful materials
- ✓ selling articles and videos
- ✓ involving publications
- ✓ photo and video reports
- ✓ customer reviews

We will talk more about each of these points in the next chapters of this book. At the same time, even if you can not figure out how to «correctly» create such content, its presence is the way to earn money. The fact is that publishing is one of the actions that help to make money. I thought what exactly is it worth publishing on social networks to attract customers and earn money? I studied and practised various ways that are designed to create posts to sell better. I noticed that when I create publications, I have customers and money. The golden rule: no publications - no customers. So I came to the conclusion that it is possible to work not only on the quality of each individual publication but also on the amount of content about my activities on the Internet. The more content there will be on the Internet — the more contacts with potential customers it will bring you.

News and stories for social networks

Write down a list of events that occur in your life or business every day. Everyone has such events.

It can be:

Meetings with customers, friends, colleagues, suppliers.

Attendance of workshops, training, courses, studies.

Going to the cinema, theatre, clubs, cafes, and concerts.

Purchases of goods, search for suppliers.

Employment of new employees.

Opening a new office.

Obtaining a certificate, diploma, certificate, license.

Making a deal

Team meeting, making a plan for the next month, a report at the end of the month on the work done.

Renewal of assortment, new services, and prices, etc.

In the modern world, there are a lot of events. Most likely, people are not aware of what is happening on the Internet. All these events you can cover in the form of news on social networks, accompanying them with interesting stories.

Of course, in some businesses, there are so many events every day and they have a repetitive nature that there is no point in talking about them every day. In this case, choose the goals to discuss and talk about. As a rule, these are your achievements and it is important to talk about them. They directly impact on your reputation and help to gain visibility.

For example, you were recognized as the best specialist in the city and had an article about you published in a magazine or got invited to the radio. This might be interesting news for different social networks.

For example, I had one of such news stories: «How Ivan Dorn bought my book». For those who don`t know who is Ivan Dorn, he is one of the most famous pops and dance music stars.

Read the story written below. This is one of the publications on my page social networks.

«The story on how Ivan Dorn bought my book :) Did I tell you that I never give my book as a present?! Today I decided to go to the library to shoot a video invitation to my workshop and accidentally I met Vanya Dorn!) I confessed how I admire him, after which we took a photo together and continued talking. I was wondering what he was doing in Odessa, how he lives, where he is hanging out. He said that he made a record at a local recording studio. I remembered my youth and told him that I also used to write music, my tracks were recorded in the studio and participated in rap battles:) In general, it was nostalgia ... Then, Ivan understood that he needed to leave, and it seemed to me somehow our meeting is illogical at the end ... I was very pleased with our conversation and wanted to give Ivan some kind of gift. I recalled I have my book «The Endless Flow of Ideas on How to Create Content for Business» with me. I wanted to give it to Vanya, but I thought that I wasn't giving this book to anyone in principle because I believed that

everyone who paid money for my book was investing some resources in the development of projects that I have been creating.

BUT Ivan Dorn is one of my favourite musicians, I am singing his songs in the shower, I even learned to play one song on my guitar :) In general, I told Ivan that I don't normally give anyone my books, but I would like to give it to him.

And he said: «So let me buy it from you. How much does it cost?». I answered that it was 10$.

Ivan said: «Well, will you give me a discount? »

Me: «Yes, of course! »

Ivan gave me 8$. I gave him a copy of my book, and, as usual, I wrote a wish and left an autograph.

I was very pleased that Ivan Dorn bought my book. He asked me to leave my phone number for communication. I do not know why, but I said that it would be very valuable for me to know his opinion about my book. I am sure that Ivan has high standards of content, which is why he makes such cool music. And I would be interested to know his opinion ... Now I'm waiting for his call and his impression about the book :)

This post received more comments and likes than others. Later, when I met different people in my city and the topic of conversation was my book, many people said: *«Well, if Ivan Dorn bought, it means that I need to buy your book too»*. It works in a very interesting way. People who you don't even know or see extremely rarely will find out such news and stories on social networks and tell them to their friends.

Useful content

Usually, when marketing specialists talk about the content in advertising, they use the words «warm up the audience» and «selling content». «Warm up the audience» means heighten someone's interest in your product or service, personality or any subject, issue, a field of activity in which you are engaged. This term is very relevant. I think you have already read about such concepts as «cold audience», «warm audience» and «hot audience».

So, the «cold audience» refers to people who know nothing about you, and working with this audience you can use the content that can «warm up» the audience, stirring the interest in your product, and introducing potential customers to your business.

You may have noticed that some actors were unknown for a long time, their fees were modest, and then one day they took part in a movie that became very popular. After that, the actor becomes known around the world. These actors have growing rows of fans as their «warm audience». Before watching that movie, looking at this actor you could have said: «just a so-so talent he has ». The audience was cold because they didn't know anything about this actor. But after one session in the cinema, having experienced various emotions and spending 90 minutes with his new character, the audience fell in love with him, the film warmed them up and the audience became «warm»

In the future, many will become fans and enjoy all the movies featuring this actor. That means that the actor himself is the reason for the sale of tickets to the cinema and not the movie.

The same story happens with the content. Movies are content too in fact. You can shoot useful video tutorials for your audience. During these videos, talk a little about yourself, your experience and achievements, the problems that you can help your clients with solving.

When you start creating your content, move in the following steps:

Make a list of topics (titles or content titles) that would be useful to your potential customers.

Choose the form in which your user content will be presented (articles, video tutorials, live broadcasts, presentations, books ...).

Make a plan for the information which will be discussed in your publication. This is usually 4–7 key points of what you want to say about the chosen topic.

Write a text, shoot a video or announce a live stream.

Create a publication on social networks.

In general, I think, everything is clear. The only thing that usually raises the concerns is the choice of topic for publication. But as soon as you choose a theme for your content, it wouldn't create any difficulties dealing with the ideas for your new useful content

Here is a couple of examples showing how to choose an interesting topic for useful content:

Write a list of questions that your customers often ask you and carry out a live stream on Facebook and Instagram with the answers to these questions.

Write a few stories on how you have helped your customers in the past. Your experience may be interesting to people.

Tell what your profession or business consists of. What kind of activity are you engaged in? Understanding your work will make it easier for clients to find specialists and solve their problems.

Make comparisons or product reviews. How to choose the goods or services you sell?

Conduct a survey among customers and find out the answers to what questions they are interested in getting. What advice would they like to get from you?

In general, any knowledge that will help your customers to benefit is regarded as useful content.

For example, I am carrying out free webinars. This is my way to create useful content. I choose an interesting topic for entrepreneurs and professionals. After the live stream, I leave the webinar record freely available so that it can be viewed at any time on my YouTube channel and on my Facebook business page.

Every entrepreneur or specialist has experience which they can share with the audience. There are senior professionals and entrepreneurs with 20–30 years of experience who might have witnessed that the old methods of advertising are already running out of efficacy, and they need to promote their services on the Internet. At the same time, it still seems to them that social networks are for young people, and they have nothing to do there. My opinion differs. And that's why... My grandmother used to tell me: «I am older than you, I have the experience, I know life, so listen to me».

Today, if you have the experience, you have an advantage. You have something to share with others, and if your children may not listen to you, your customers will do. Children think that they themselves know how to live, and they rarely ask for advice from the older generation. Clients, on the contrary, need advice and help. They always have questions that they often have no one to help with.

There are many people in the world who need your help. Just be helpful.

For example, when dealing with the real estate industry, I worked with a company, led by Kristina Zvereva. We organized workshops for her on how to invest in real estate in Odessa for potential buyers willing to purchase an apartment in newly-built residential complexes. This workshop was definitely useful, as it helped people to better understand how to choose an apartment, how to save money or make money on real estate, how to choose an apartment of good quality. Kristina, as a realtor, knew all the pitfalls of this work and spoke about them during those events. We decided that this information would be useful to find out not only at live events but also on the Internet. We started recording all the new workshops on video and created useful videos for social networks that anyone could watch.

I have already said that events and content are inextricably linked. Perhaps there are certain events in your business that can benefit your customers. These can be meetings and negotiations, product presentations, selection and sorting of goods, search for suppliers and so on. All these events can be digitized, captured on video, photos, and used in the process of creating useful content for social networks.

When you begin to create useful and interesting publications on social networks, you will notice that the audience will become «warmer». People will ask you questions more often in comments, write private messages and ask for advice. From now, selling your goods and services becomes easier for you.

"Selling" content

Usually, when tunning the ads to target a new audience, we use only a few types of content to attract customers:

photos of goods with an attractive (selling) text in the description.

Selling articles with a banner.

marketer videos and selling text in the description.

I believe that these three types of content are perhaps the most important in attracting customers through advertising on Facebook and Instagram. Often it's enough to shoot one advertising video, run advertising and get hundreds of customers.

The amount of money that you spend on advertising and the number of new clients will depend on how much this content will influence the audience targeted by the advertising on social networks. Here is an example, once we have set up an advertising campaign for an amusement park in Odessa. Potential customers were parents with children and teenagers. My student – an advertising manager with insignificant experience – was responsible for that campaign. He set up advertising on Facebook and Instagram according to my recommendations. By the time he passed my training, he knew a lot about the structure of selling texts. We discussed with him everything he needed to know about the target audience and the promotion strategy.

So, a few days after the launch of advertising, we began receiving contacts of first potential customers. To analyze the effectiveness of advertising, we made a preliminary report, from which it became clear that the cost of a potential client was high since every contact (got through lead-magnet strategy) cost about 2$.

In general, this is a nice price, but I understood that it was possible to improve the results. Therefore, I asked the manager to turn off personalized ads temporarily. I have re-written my own selling article for the target audience and made a new, more attractive banner for the advertising campaign. Then we launched the advertising campaign to a narrower audience. I chose the option in the settings to target «only people aged 20 to 40 from Odessa who have birthdays in June».

On the same day, we saw how the statistics changed. The cost of attracting a potential client has decreased by 20 times. Now, one lead contact was costing 0.10$. What did we change? What is the difference? Why did the indicators change so much when re-setting up the advertising?

My student and me, we used similar pictures and the same banner headline. But thanks to my experience, I have already learned to observe styles, choose more beautiful fonts and place the text on the picture so that it attracts more attention and looks more expensive. I also chose a more accurate audience on Facebook, those who were shown ads. I have excluded the audiences for whom my offer was irrelevant.

These were the tiny nuances, but they allowed us to reduce the cost of attracting customers by 20 times. And this is the result. To create extremely effective content for business, you need experience. But even if you have no experience, my recommendations will help you to make the result better than what you have now, and most importantly, to make it consciously.

Over time, when you accumulate a certain experience, you will make your selling content more effective. But you have to sell already now! So, I decided to give you a structure of marketer texts. This is the perfect plan according to which your publications should be created.

Here are a few questions to help you create a selling text for your article or video:

- What is your offer? What do you offer and for whom is it relevant?
- What are the benefits of using the product?
- What kind of problems does it solve? In what situation is it worth to buy it?
- What is the product, service or event? What are the stages of the work?
- Appeal for the action. What should be done right now to place an order? Add some links, phone numbers and other ways to contact you.
- Introduce yourself. Tell about yourself, your company and work experience.

Select the product, service or event for which you want to write a marketer text. Ask yourself these questions about your product. This will be your plan - what your marketer text for advertising will consist of.

Here is an example to make it clearer.

The product: women's evening dresses.

The clients: women aged 20–35 years.

Question 1: What is your proposal? What do you suggest and for whom is it relevant?

Answer 1: Ladies, Check these female evening dresses. The new models are perfect for any date with your sweethearts.

Question 2: What are the benefits of using the product?

Answer 2: In this dress, you will look stunning, everyone will be staring at you.

Question 3: What kind of problems does it solve? In what situation is it worth to buy it?

Answer 3: The dress will highlight your beautiful hourglass figure, show and emphasize your curves. I recommend it to everyone who has a full wardrobe, but nothing to wear.

Question 4: What is the product, service or event? What are the stages of the work?

Answer 4: The dress is made from pleasant natural fabric (here you can specify the name of the fabric, type). It is red. All sizes are available. Before buying, you can come to our showroom and try it on or order it online, and we will arrange the delivery.

Question 5: Appeal for the action. What should be done right now to place an order? Add links, phone number and other ways to contact you.

Answer 5: To place an order, write me a personal message here: (link). I'll help you select your size. You can also call by phone (phone number). After placing the order, it will be sent by mail to any city.

Question 6: Introduce yourself. Tell us about yourself, your company, work experience.

Answer 6: My name is Mary, add me as a friend we will communicate. I've been designing and selling brand clothes for 4 years, I have a store.

It's OK? Does it work? I want to say right away that this text was invented for this book, and I did not try to use it as an advertisement. But according to this structure, I wrote over 1000 articles for various goods, services, and events. With the selling texts, I helped my clients sell products worth more than $100,000 on the Internet. Of course, you will say something like «It's great Alex, but it's clear with regard to selling dresses, but what about services or educational activities?»

It's actually still easier here. Take a sheet of paper and a pen. Have you taken? OK, write:

My product. What am I selling?

My target customer. Who do I offer my product to? Who can benefit using it?

The structure. Answer the questions I wrote for you above. Also write down the answers on a piece of paper, as I did for you in the example with the women's dress.

That's all! Now, when you have your marketer text for advertising on social networks, all you have to do is add a photo or a banner and set up advertising on Facebook and Instagram on the target client. When I say «set up advertisements», I mean make your advertising is seen to your potential customers and not just anyone. There is nothing difficult. You will only need to select gender, age, a city of residence and the interests of your potential customers in the settings.

You can learn more about the possibilities of advertising on Facebook and Instagram in one of the chapters of this book. So, it`s clear what your selling advertising text should consist of, I can tell you that you can use the same text to create a marketing video. When you have a marketer text, just learn it and record the video where you pronounce this text on the camera. **There are several** nuances of shooting selling videos, and let's talk about them.

Decide on the equipment for shooting your video. Some of us, of course, shoot the videos using own smartphone. This option is better than nothing. Ideally, of course, shoot a video using professional equipment.

Select a location. Where will you shoot the video? The place should be beautiful and convey the energy of your activities. If you sell dresses, it could be your showroom, restaurant or a private house with a pool. Make sure that the location is bright enough for the video to be bright.

How do you look on camera? Put on the clothes in which you look like a professional. Make a hairstyle.

The duration of the video. Decide in advance how long the video should be. For advertising on Instagram, for example, there is a limit of 1 minute. I think you can handle it. There is nothing complicated about it. If you need help, find a videographer, photographer, makeup artist, hairdresser, stylist, or just a friend who will support you in everything.

Now that you know the fundamentals of creating marker texts and videos, let's talk about publishing your selling content on your personal page in the news feed.

It should be published together with news and useful materials, entertainment stories and photos of your life. When your content is geared towards only direct sales to people, it can be just annoying for your subscribers. Their activity will decrease. It is necessary to alternate between useful content and selling content. Posting selling content only is normal in advertising, but not on the personal pages, where people add you as a friend to communicate with you, and not to watch what you sell them.

Customer reviews

Every business should have customer reviews. Usually, when I am dealing with business projects, I almost always make 3-5 video reviews with the clients. I will tell you how it usually works.

For example, let's take my work with the company "The World of Ladders", that manufactures ladders for multi-level houses and apartments. The business owner's name is Andrey, we worked with him for several months on promoting their online business.

It turned out that during those 17 years of activity, the company had been working with many different people, and one of the clients was Nonna Grishaeva. She is a famous theatre and cinema actress in Ukraine. We understood that her review would be valuable for the company.

«The World of Ladders» made ladders and doors for her house. We had something to show and tell about the work done. Andrey contacted Nonna and she agreed to shoot a video.

The only issue was that Nonna lived in Moscow, and me, I was living Odessa, yet we organized a lot of work despite the distance. So, don`t worry if your customers are in another city or another country. You can organize this work as we did, the way I have done it many times already.

I contacted Nonna through Viber. We discussed the details of the shooting. I told her that I had found a videographer in Moscow, who would come to the theatre and shoot 5–10 minutes of video. On the same day, I sent her a list of questions covering what we would like to know. I have written the list of these questions below.

Questions to the client for a video review:

Introduce yourself. What is your name? Where are you from? What is your hobby (activity, work)?

What was the product you bought from us? When the purchase took place? Who helped you with the purchase?

What problems were you dealing with before the purchase? Why have you decided to buy our product?

Tell about the work`s stages? Tell us more about what we have done for you.

What was the result you got? Were there some emotions, events happened in your life after purchasing our product?

Your wishes. What do you want to advise people who are in the same situation?

Usually, these questions are enough for a review to be as complete as possible, establish credibility and reveal the essence of work with the client. Then I contacted that videographer in Moscow brought him up to date and gave technical tasks for work.

To shoot a video review you need:

- Camera. The video must be of good quality.
- Tripod. The frame must be static.
- Lavalier. To record high-quality sound.
- Location. It is necessary to choose a place where the client will sit or stand. The place where the interview will take place should be beautiful.

- Medium shot. It is necessary to record in such a way that the speaker is visible from the waist and up.

- Lighting fixtures. If the room is dark, you need to turn on all possible sources of light. But if this is not enough - you can put additional light sources.

- Shoot extra backstage frames. Show the location where everything happens. Show the customer and your product. You can also use this technical task to work with videographers and create video reviews.

When everything was ready, we set the date, time and place of shooting. I was in another city at that moment. When the shooting ended, the videographer contacted me and said that everything was fine. On the same day, he sent me all the video materials in a file, and I paid for his services using an online payment system. I watched the video, it was great.

We also organized a video shooting in the house of Nonna Grisheva. We wanted to show all the work that «The World of Ladders» company has done for the client. I asked the videographer to shoot the client's house, stairs from different angles and doors. These were the frames that we wanted to use as a backstage for Nonna's interview.

When all materials were filmed, the only task left was to select good frames, cut the picture, add the background music, titles, and the company logo, and I hired a video editor for that.

Here is the technical task that I gave to the video editor:

- Select good frames and cut the interview to show the client speech is integral and logical.
- During the interview add some backstage frames.
- Add some music. Make it quiet and background. It is important that it doesn't have copyright, otherwise, your videos may be blocked on YouTube.
- Add captions. Specify the name of the client, activity.
- Add the animated company logo at the end of the video.
- Carry out the colour correction of the video.
- Save the file in FullHD and send it to me.

When the review of Nonna Grishaeva was already fully prepared, we uploaded this video to the YouTube channel, Facebook, and added it to the website of «The World of Ladders». You might think that it is too much work to do to get just one review. If it is still difficult for you to make video reviews, you can ask customers to write a text review, create it and publish it on your pages on social networks and on the website. To do this, send questions to your client, which were mentioned above, and ask to honestly write their opinion about their experience working with you.

Reviews establish trust on the Internet. There are already more than 70 video reviews of clients on my YouTube channel. And when people ask me if I have some feedback from previous clients, I usually show those reviews. Of course, many avoid checking those reviews, yet their availability closes any possible trust concerns.

Here is a couple of reasons why I never bought reviews:

- ✓ Real reviews give you real feedback. Real people who have had the experience of interacting with you and your product, and returned to give their feedback, will help you grow professionally.

✓ Customer reviews are your personal history. This is the content that will be relevant for ages. And if you really love your business, in 5–10 years you will be pleased to see the reviews from your first customers and remember how it started.

✓ It`s true. The purpose of reviews is trust and recommendations. Why would you use fake reviews, if that can only affect the client's trust in your business?

These reviews will help you run the jungle telegraph on the Internet. How does it work? A client addressed to you, and later you asked him to recommend your company to other people. The customer is gone. And you just can't control how the jungle telegraph worked further. At the same time, if you shot a video review with this client, you yourself control how many recommendations your client will make to people. You can publish this review online and show it through advertising to potential customers. So you can independently start the jungle telegraph.

But what can you do if your clients refuse to leave reviews, or you are just starting your business and you haven`t got a lot of clients yet? Ask your friends to become your customers. Ask them to use your products or services, become customers of your business, and then shoot your friends' review. Do not lie. Tell the truth. Let your friend say that you asked him to leave a review of your company. Let a friend tell the real story about how they became your client, tried the product and share their opinion about it. Do not try to make your review look perfect, make it honest and it will establish credibility on the Internet. So you will be credible.

Photo and video reviews of events.

There are certain events that make sense to carry out only for the purpose of getting the photo and video reports. For example, the presentation of my first book in Odessa. I published a book, and I could present it on social networks. But I thought it is important to make a presentation in the library, gather people, sign autographs, make photos and videos at the event. Later, I occasionally used those photos and videos from this presentation on social networks, presentations during workshops, live streams and videos on YouTube.

Now, just imagine that I would not have these materials. This event would remain only in the heads of its participants: in my memory, in the memory of those who were with me at the presentation. Only these people could confirm the fact that the presentation was real.

After the presentation of the book, I travelled to different cities across Ukraine and carried out workshops, where I always mentioned that I was the author of the book and I had a presentation in Odessa. But what if I didn't have a photo of this event? How could people believe me? I also did not have books with me.

Photo and video reports prove that there were certain events in your business and you can share them. Now, recall the events in your professional activity that you are proud of.

Perhaps the first courses where you were trained to become a specialist. Or diploma delivery ceremony or getting a certificate of excellence. Or you have implemented a large project that you would like to show people on the Internet today. But you have nothing to show. These are the events that remain only in your memory. People may never be able to see and experience what once happened in your life on the Internet. Today, you have no opportunity to share this with your friends on social networks.

It's like a photo and video made at the birth of a child, or your graduation at school or university or your wedding. Do you have these family videos? So why don't you have such videos for your business? Your business is also a part of your life, which you will be proud of after many years. So, keep making photo and video reports.

Here are some recommendations on how to organize a photo or video report:

> ➢ Find a photographer / videographer.
> ➢ Discuss shooting date, time.
> ➢ Discuss the event plan.

For example, you are a specialist in apartment remodelling and want to take photos and videos about your work for a major client. Discuss the work schedule with the photographer/videographer. Tell the details of your work. For example:

- Negotiating the project details with the client,
- creation of drawings and 3D design of the apartment,
- purchase of construction materials
- apartment remodelling
- furnishing
- housing.

All these stages are what your event, project or chain of events consists of. It is important to discuss everything with the photographer and video operator so that they are aware of how much time it will take and can understand approximately the scope of work on photo and video.

Discuss which shoots should be taken during the event. You can ask the specialist to write you a list of shoots that could be taken. So you will be able to evaluate the work in advance and understand what to expect as a result.

Find out what equipment will be used for taking photos and videos.

Introduce the photographer and videographer to the person responsible for your event. Agree on the date, time and place where you will have to meet, and how much time the event and the shooting will need. After the shooting, I recommend you to copy all the shoots and videos to a separate data storage device and then pay for photo and video specialist services.

All the photos and videos should be then processed by the photographer/operator, including colour correction and editing.

Can you imagine how many photos and videos for your business will you have if you make at least a few photo reports of projects and events? You will have hundreds, and maybe thousands of photos and videos that you can later use for various publications on social networks.

Involvement

It is important for me that people interact with me. I have seen entrepreneurs who have used black-hat techniques to get 100,000 subscribers on Instagram, yet their publications were bringing like 100 likes and several comments. This is an example of bad audience involvement.

Here are some ways to help you engage with your audience on social networks:

✓ Carry out opinion polls
✓ Organize live events, meetings, presentations for clients.
✓ Come up and carry out promotions with very cool gifts or discounts.
✓ Create publications and respond to comments.
✓ Record Stories.
✓ Carry out live streams.
✓ Create chats and chat with people in closed communities.
✓ Discuss ideas and implement new projects with customers.

Why do you need it? From the point of view of social networks, if your subscribers underreact to your publications, it means they are not interesting to them. And thus, they will be less likely to be shown by Facebook and Instagram in the news feed. In other words, if you have 1000 subscribers, then only 100 of them will see your post. That is why the number of subscribers often isn't very important. If involvement is low, a few people will see your content.

This is only a technical side of the issue. I think about it a little differently. People who are not involved in your business, in your life, will forget about you as soon as they unsubscribe from your pages on social networks. And this question interests me much more. The exposure of your publications might be increased. If your posts have few views, you can set up advertisements so that thousands of people can see them. But if the content and the subject you are writing about in your posts do not resonate, don't catch public attention, this is much worse, in my opinion.

Recall your friends or colleagues. Most likely, you will think about those with whom you spent a lot of time together, with whom you had bright events and memories. Some stories that you never forget. These stories are the result of important interactions in your life. People on the Internet don't think that you are real. You do not bring any emotions, they don't write to you, don't ask questions. If you don`t communicate with people on the Internet every day, it means that you are not very involved.

Personal brand

For some reason, the participants in our workshops and my clients began asking me about a personal brand. It was strange for me because I didn`t tell anyone that I understand and provide services in this field of activity. But apparently, the people who surround me noticed that those with whom I've been working became better-known experts and their client base increased. People also talk about me and, apparently, I show by my example how to develop a personal brand, although, frankly speaking, I never persuaded such a goal. Well, or I never called it a «personal brand». I have just been creating content for business and implementing interesting online projects.

Your personal brand is really important because people want to buy from trusted people and companies. Your potential customers call their friends and ask them to recommend a good specialist or company because it isn`t always easy to find such people on the Internet. Have you tried today to find a plumber to fix something in your house?

Or an electrician? I really do not understand how can I find such a person on the Internet. I can find many phone numbers of plumbers on the Internet, but I absolutely don't know anything about these people and I don't know if I can trust them. I would like to see a specialist who has his Instagram account, where he shows photos of his family, his photos at work. I could see customer reviews and useful tips on taking care of household appliances. Thus, I would know that this person is not afraid of publicity. Their openness to social networks would tell me a lot and bring more trust.

Now I will *reveal a secret* and lay everything on the line, I will discuss how I develop my personal brand with the help of content.

I am convinced that if a business or a person who wants to promote own brand is «a piece of shit (I apologize for the coarse words) », then neither advertising nor content would shape them up into goodness, at least in my experience. This piece can only grow to become «Hotspur» on the Internet, which people will talk about.

All I am trying to do in my work is to find features in the business, in goods, services, and events that I like and show them on the Internet. All of them. If you as a person are of no great shakes, your personal brand will be the same.

That is why I recommend you to work on the development of the personality, and then on the brand. Develop skills that make you the best specialist, reveal the deep qualities of a good person in your heart, change your restrictive beliefs to positive ones.

Your brand is an impression that shows your company or yourself to consumers. If you make an unpleasant impression when meeting people in life, people wouldn't trust you. If you annoy people more than interest, then by promoting your «personal brand», you will simply increase the number of negative thoughts around you.

Of course, there are large companies that carry out large-scale research, and they employ dozens of marketing experts, who are engaged in the development of the personal brand. But these companies also ensure that their actions on the market do not contradict with their brand. For example, take the Coca-Cola Company. They have strict standards. The first thing I think about when I hear «Coca-Cola» is: «We bring you happiness and joy». This is their brand. Moreover, all actions that can bring misfortune are limited. A friend of mine who works for a waste management company told me once that Coca-Cola is one of the companies in Ukraine for which they set the most stringent standards for the destruction of expired products.

At the same time, Coca-Cola strongly supports and participates in events that bring joy. Gosh, they came up with the legendary Santa Claus ads. In essence, they have introduced a tradition and event into the culture of several generations, which brings joy to people all over the world. Do you understand what I mean?

As I said, first come to the events, then comes the content. First of all, become a person, followed by others, and then show your brand on the Internet.

I understand, perhaps, comparing yourself with a multi-billion dollar company, you will feel yourself too small and you may lose the motivation for self-development, so I will bring you an example. What do I do to develop a personal brand?

I create events and achievements in those fields which I am interested in. And talk about it. For example, everyone is talking about education in the country, that it needs to be changed, but in fact, a few people do something to make it happen. From 2016 to 2018, I gave about 40 lectures in Ukrainian universities engaging more than a thousand students. I was a member of the jury in an advertising competition for students in the city of Odessa. I was a part of the committee during the graduation exams for a master's degree in marketing. I asked them questions that would help them in their development.

I surveyed more than 300 students to understand their interests, and subsequently, these questionnaires gave me more insight into how teens are taught. Based on these questionnaires, several training workshops and courses for students were created. I did it because I wanted to develop the education system in my country. Because I am learning something new every day and it is interesting for me to develop this field. Think about what achievements you could create in your field of work in order to improve your position in society and the position of others. It should be something, you have never done before. Something that will help you become better and prove to yourself that you can pursue more ambitious goals.

Make a list of these desired achievements. And achieve your goals. Then, simply stream all these achievements on the Internet. Show what you have achieved. Speak about the achievements you are in the process of reaching. Just create your personal content. That's all. If you already have achievements, start by telling about them on social networks and on your website. Show letters, awards, medals, photos, and videos of the projects you've done that you are proud of.

I know many experts and businessmen with more than 15 years of experience on the market, and their websites «About the Company» section features only 5 lines of text. I don`t believe that you haven`t got any achievements in your field of work. You have been working for ages. I think you have something to tell people.

Frequency of publications

The frequency of publications is directly related to the number of events occurring in the business. I have already said that your social networking pages are a reflection of your life and work. How fast are you progressing? How often do you have something new? That's exactly the frequency you should create new posts with.

For example, in the area of clothes sales, you can get new items and collections every day. There are seasonal sales and new collections. It is really necessary to inform people on the Internet about all these changes and events.

In the info business, with some well-coordinated work on hand, you can train your clients every day and carry out workshops every month. So, when recruiting people to join your workshop, you should notify potential participants on the Internet in advance, so that they can plan their time and prepare money for the training. That`s why I recommend writing one post every day.

In the service niche, it all depends on how busy you are. If you own a beauty salon, have 20 customers every day, purchase necessary tools 2 times a month, participate in workshops once in every 6 months, you can show the examples of your work every day, talk about the tools you work with several times a month, show the diplomas, certificates from the courses you took part in and etc.

When people ask me how should they post on social networks, I respond: «And how often do events happen in your business?» Some, answering this question, say that they have a few events. If you have nothing to tell about, you should not fill up the lack of events in life with excessive publications on the Internet. Create new events and show them on the social network.

Do not forget to live.

I think that Facebook and Instagram have become an important part of our life and business, but it's definitely not worth spending your life on social networks.

I would say, fill your life with interesting events so that there is something to show and tell on Facebook and Instagram.

You are entrepreneurs, and you have your business to develop. If social networks take a lot of time, create a new position in your company and let a specialist do it. You already have everything you need to delegate these processes. You have this book on hand. Just read it to the end to learn about all the possibilities of promotion on social networks. It doesn't matter whether you yourself are engaged in the promotion on Facebook and Instagram or you delegate these tasks because this book will help you make more effective decisions. Just read it to the end.

Other than that, if you are an entrepreneur, you have a business and your field of activity isn`t connected with marketing, but you are only interested in promoting your products and services, of course, you don't have to waste your life on posts and likes. Do not try to please everyone on the Internet. Just live.

Live so that there is something to show on the Internet. Just create events in your life and business, and then show them on the network. Broadcast all the time. Create super content. Show photos and videos, tell stories to your subscribers.

I understand that life goes on. And I would definitely not like to live in front of a computer. Don't forget that when your life comes to an end, all the likes and comments will not be as important for future generations as your achievements and events that you created for your environment, clients, relatives.

Practical task:

- Shape up your personal page.
- Create and shape up a business page.
- Shoot 3 customer video reviews.
- Create photo and video reports of important events in your business.
- Determine the frequency of new posts.
- Write a list of planned events in your business for the next month, quarter, year, and schedule the publication of news for these events.
- Carry out several useful live streams.

Chapter 3

ATTRACTING CUSTOMERS FROM INSTAGRAM

Igor OSETSIMSKIY

The Indian ritual «Nahua» ("Why the fcuk")

Most likely, by now you have already understood that you should be present on social networks, including Instagram to run your business successfully. Let`s talk about the reason to start an Instagram business account and, of course, how to use it to get a stream of customers.

I believe the biggest mistake entrepreneurs usually make is that they know they should have an account on Instagram, but don't start it because they don`t know how to promote their account on the Internet.

I think everyone knows that Instagram is a huge source of income, especially in modern life realia. Most likely, you have already created your account and are dealing with the following difficulties: you don't have any subscribers, no one likes your posts, you got just a few orders and most likely you are disappointed because you have already written quality content, and even made professional photos and published a lot of posts. Yet no feedback or clients showed up. And here comes the disappointment because you don't know what to do to boost your sales through Instagram.

Just imagine, Instagram already has more than 1 billion users. More than five hundred million users log in to Instagram every day. For example, according to the 2017 statistics, there are more than 5 million active Instagram users only across Ukraine. The pace Instagram is growing with is ten times higher than that of Facebook. In 2017, the number of views of videos on Instagram grew by 80% compared with the previous year. More than 2 million large-scale advertisers use Instagram. Among them, there are BMW, Mercedes, and others.

Benefits of using a business Instagram account:

-   quick access to a product or service. With just one click a client can contact you (write a message, call, leave a comment);

-   easy to create trusting relationships. You assure you are a real person through posting awesome photos, posts, and videos.

-   you don`t even need to create a quality website. It means you don`t need to contact a designer and a programmer because you can do everything on your own.

The main idea that I would like to bring you is that you need to create and develop your personal brand, in the first place. It is important. And you need to do everything in such a way so that people will begin to know and understand what you are doing. Most likely, you will say: «Why should I write this, everyone already knows what I am doing». But it`s far from it. They don`t know! 60,000 people are subscribed to my personal account. You know, I have been «collecting» the subscribers for three long years.

They have followed me most probably because they already knew what I have been doing. But even now, when I ask people if they know what I am doing, not everyone has an affirmative reply. And this is despite the fact that I have mentioned all my activities in my profile, which is advertising, promotion of social networks, website development. I indicated that I am the owner of the Internet marketing agency, "Verona". But still – not everyone is aware! No matter what your segment is: B2B or B2C, you definitely need to get into P2P – in People to People. Because the more sincere and honest you will be with your subscribers, the quicker they can become your clients.

People are interested in observing people. What do you do, how do you relax, what is your hobby, what do you eat, what kind of family do you have, how do you build relationships, how emotional are you, what do you do in your free time, what kind of car do you drive, what kind of sport do you like, who do you communicate with, how are your friends, how are your relationships with your parents and so on.

It doesn't matter what products or services you offer, what secret mechanisms are used — just write about them. If you have a cool idea — write about it. I can assure you that your idea will not be stolen for the reason that you are the first to talk about it. Even if you are a top-notch restaurateur, you can safely share the secrets of cooking. No one will steal your idea. And even if they do, don`t worry. After all, you are already the first one to tell the world about it.

Moreover, you will be considered a leader in this field. An expert. It is enough just to talk about simple things, and you will be considered an expert.

For example, we have a client. This is a woman who is engaged in the real estate business. She is a realtor. And she started posting on Instagram about how to buy real estate, what documents to have, how to pay money and how to carry it out safely. These are the ordinary simple things, and the things that everyone might know. But due to the fact that it was her to explain this, she is now considered an expert in this field, and if someone needs to buy an apartment, they would first ask her. They will contact her because for them she knows the process better.

Believe it or not, but it was you who began considering me an expert on Instagram because I began to explain simple banal things. For example: «To start an account on Instagram, you need to have a smartphone», «Install the Instagram application on the phone» "You will need a profile pic and logo when setting up your account", etc. I only talked about this, and they began to contact me with promotion questions. I shared the information with one potential client, and he later recommended me to another, then to the third one, and so on.

These clients got a result, and they started recommending me as an expert. Moreover, it was they who made me an expert, they asked me questions, I found the answers on the Internet, looking for insiders who could help me.

If I wasn't able to find the answers, I went to buy training courses. I asked the team members to help me find the necessary information. And so, I have been gaining knowledge. But it all started with the fact that I just talked about simple things.

For example, you are selling clothes or shoes on the Internet. Here, people need to know how to choose the right shirt (dress, skirt, pants), the right size, how to not get mistaken with it when buying clothes online, what happens if the ordered shoes are not of the correct size. Only then people will start considering you an expert in this area. And they will begin to recommend you and your store.

Instagram is like a snowball because the more information you give, the more live streams you create, the more products or services you introduce to your subscribers, the more contacts you will end up getting.

Here is what I have to tell you. For the past three years, I have not given any advertising at all just because 3 years ago I shaped up my Instagram account pretty nice. That is why more and more new clients keep coming, without any advertising. There are some marketing strategies of course, as I carefully plan what I will post, where I will speak, what kind of clients I would like to have. I use other resources, but I am enjoying the process of running my Instagram.

So how do you start promoting your Instagram account?

From the age of 16, I was looking for my predestination. I gained diverse Vedic knowledge and was fond of Indian culture. I once read that Steve Jobs went to India trying to find harmony with his inner self. I also believed that only in India you can understand your destiny. Meditate, communicate with monks, cut your hair, and live in the mountains. I had a dream to travel to India for a month and live there without a phone or any gadget and make my dream of finding my predestination come true. At that time, I did not have the financial means to fulfil this dream. Therefore, I found different meditations, mentors who helped me find myself without travelling to other countries. I listened to positive affirmations and meditations, did yoga-exercises. Once I got to hear about this Indian ritual called «Nahua» ("Why the fcuk").

Before starting any serious and difficult work, it is very useful to carry out this secret Indian ritual, «Nahua». It lies in the fact that an Indian usually seriously asks himself: «Is this work an expression of the deep aspirations of my heart? Do I really want this? Will I be happy when I realize my plans? Will I be happy when I will do everything that I have to do? Will my dreams come true? Is this goal worth the money to spend? »

And then, the first thing I ask myself is "Nahua (Whythefcuk)" I need that?" Okay, just kidding here, I am asking myself who are my clients and why should they buy my services.

Here are some questions that might help you on certain occasions:

✓ When you ask yourself «Who is my ideal client? », you create an image of a person whom you will be comfortable working with. Believe me, if you have a lot of customers who screw your brain up, you will not get any pleasure from your business. You will only spend your energy not for creation and development, but for settling relations!

As soon as you understand who your ideal client is, you will most likely experience a sense of gratitude and satisfaction, and you will realize that you are carrying something valuable into this world.

✓ By answering the question: «Why should a client buy my services? », you understand what advantages you have over your competitors, understand your strongest points, and therefore you can always improve your business.

How to create and shape up your account on Instagram

Once you have answered these questions, you just need to proceed to the creation of your account. And it is not difficult. You only need to pay attention to these five points:

- profile photo;
- business profile;
- marketing description;
- contacts;
- posting.

Profile photo

The first thing you need to do is to make a profile photo. It's not difficult, but there are a few rules to follow to make it beautiful, so that thanks to your profile photo, more people subscribe to your profile.

Here are the rules. As long as you are not Apple and Adidas (your business is currently unknown and you are not yet known at the market), it does not make sense to cling to your logo on your avatar. If, for example, you are engaged in the market of clothes, choose a gorgeous girl in a beautiful dress or beautiful shoes you are actually selling for your profile photo.

If you are engaged in technology, make a profile photo with a girl taking a selfie. If you own a beauty salon, the pic might be featuring a pretty girl holding a phone in her freshly manicured fingers. Even if you have opened your restaurant, make a pic of a pretty girl eating delicious food. If you are known within your city or region, then it makes sense to put your logo on the avatar. It will be great for restaurants, coffee houses, etc.

If you are promoting a business through your personal brand, I recommend choosing blue or violet background for your photo. For me, these colours express the brightest activity. The colours actually change every year, so you will have to test them. I will discuss colour testing strategies later.

Hereby, I can say these two colours bring me the maximum number of subscribers. When choosing the blue colour, you should not contact the designer, just take a picture of the background of a swimming pool.

Business profile

So, you have registered your account, but you need to transfer it to a business profile. After having this done, you will have the opportunity to track the statistics, add more characters to the profile description, add the advertisement right from your smartphone.

To do this, simply go to the Instagram settings and select the option «switch to a business profile».

Description

Your profile description is a very important part of sales! It is vital to describe here who you are, what your activity is, and how you work. Don`t forget to indicate how to contact you. Also, I recommend using smilies in the description. No matter how serious you think your business is, no matter how serious you look like, the conversion says that the performance is always higher when you don't use the plain text only. Consequently, people will be more interested in you and you will be able to keep the attention of potential subscribers only after you add emoticons.

At the end of the description, add your appeal for action and promise to give subscribers something in return for subscribing to your account. This may be a checklist, free consultation or discount, there may be free measurements, and so on.

The call for action must be changed regularly. Just try. By doing this, you can get several times more subscribers.

Examples of appeals:

- ✓ Subscribe and get a discount.
- ✓ Subscribe and I will audit your account.
- ✓ Subscribe and I will analyze your business.
- ✓ Subscribe and I will present you a book.

It is very important to indicate the advantages of your services in the description. Use concise yet catchy means of describing the benefits that you can give to your potential customers. For example:

- ✓ I can bring a stream of customers
- ✓ I can offer to coach
- ✓ I can create a brand
- ✓ I can earn billions for companies.

Most common mistakes that can be made in your description:

- • We have the best product.
- • We offer only quality goods.
- • We offer free shipping, etc.

Are there any businessmen who believe that their product is worse or defective? None! All the entrepreneurs are sure they have the best product. You will never meet someone who sells goods and says that they offer a piece of trash, but the price is good or the product is defective but cheap. Nobody says that.

It is better to write about the advantages. For example, if you mention that you offer free food delivery, this is not an advantage. Nowadays, many companies are offering free delivery and, due to this, the consumer is convinced that the delivery should be free.

Do not waste the space mentioning obvious things in the description. Fill this empty space with your perks. It is not necessary to include a lot of phone numbers. Only one is enough.

Contacts

It is important to make it easy for your potential clients to contact you: through a Direct message, call, or another messenger. Also, it is vital - even if you do not have an office or a work address, indicate the geo-mark of your location. No one will check it, but this way, you will get additional rank on Google search engine.

Posts

After completing all of the above-mentioned steps, you will need to develop a strategy for your publications, stories, and live streams.

The starting point is your first posts. It does not matter if your account has been registered a long time ago or just recently. Introduce yourself, your services or goods to all potential customers. Describe yourself and your journey: tell who you are, what do you do, how you came to where you are now. Tell your story. Create 3–6 posts about it. This will be your starting point. You should understand that the content is the most important part because 70% of the success depends on what posts you are making.

The steps to create quality posts:

1. Always start your post with a headline asking your subscribers a question. Thanks to this question, you encourage people to start reading your publication. If there is a lot of text, another question is needed in the middle of the text. Thus, you will again attract the attention of the reader. And it is important! Ask questions at the end of the post, but

as an appeal for action. For example, you can write what you think about a certain thing or etc; or write, how it happened with you, or specify in the comments under this post how you act in that certain case. Thus, the question should be drafted in such a way that the subscriber wants to comment on it. Below I will explain why this is important.

2. Write the question right on the photo you are using for the post, but don't do it with every post, otherwise, it will repel your readers.

3. Use different smilies in your posts, it will also attract the subscribers, and the text will not seem boring.

4. After each 3–5 lines start a new paragraph by using «Enter».

5. Add hashtags. At least five under each post and every time interchange the position of them and also add some new ones.

How to develop a strategy for your posts?

To develop a correct posting strategy, first of all, carry out the following actions:

✓ Define the TSA (target audience)

- ✓ Find your competitors and check what they write about.
- ✓ Make a list of things you can write about. And make another list of things you have experience in.
- ✓ Make a list of topics which are interesting for you.
- ✓ Make a list of topics which are relevant on the Internet as of present.
- ✓ Highlight 7 directions for your content: entertaining, expert, personal, working, facts, innovations, self-development, etc.
- ✓ Proceeding from the answers, go with your gut instincts and define what content you will publish.
- ✓ Create a schedule for your publications for the next week. Plan your publications carefully.

Quality photos

I know many of you, and myself too, have faced the following problem: you have enough ideas to write about, but you don't have high-quality photos. But there is a solution. Instagram is very flexible and you can make high-quality photographs without any designers. Instagram was initially created as a tool for processing and editing photos. It had to simply save people from having to contact the designer every time before posting a photo. The meaning of creating Instagram is to solve the problem of poor-quality photos. I believe that the creators succeeded in their mission.

Every smartphone has a camera today. You just have to ask someone to snap your picture. Although even without any help you can do the following: take a selfie over a cup of coffee or while walking in the park. Yes, now you can take pictures using your phone without any expensive equipment and technology.

Among my clients, there are many restaurant owners and we don`t hire professional photographers, we only use our iPhones. To get a beautiful photo, you just have to lay out your clothes or food on a table, and add an aromatic and cosy cup of coffee/latte/ cappuccino. If you do not sell, but provide services, it is enough to photograph yourself in a suitable setting and perspective.

It is very important to pay attention to the background. The background should maximally reflect the interests of your target audience. For example, if these are students, there should be a blackboard or flipchart in the background. If you are the owner of a fitness centre and sell seasonal passes, just take a photo outside of the gym.

If you understand that you need macro photography (close-up photography of objects), it is enough to purchase additional lenses to the built-in camera, which are commercially available and easily connected to the phone.

Using the photo editing function of Instagram you can easily adjust the brightness, contrast, details and sharpness. Don't you think now that everything is much simpler than you initially thought?

Money and popularity on Instagram

After you have shaped up your account, developed a posting strategy, built your full positioning, you need to think about how to make sales. What should you do to become popular?

At this stage, you need to invest in your subscribers. This means being as useful as possible to them. It is necessary to find a way to attract even more audience and think about how you can interact with those who are already subscribed to you.

You seriously need to think about traffic. Traffic is the flow of visitors to your account. It is recommended to contact specialists or study and try to promote your account on your own.

In order to stir the interest of the audience, you need to deal with the content of your account. This is an entire marketing strategy. Although, on the other hand, it is enough just to show everything you do and go through along the day. And that's all.

Discuss which seminars you attend, which exhibitions you should visit, what event to take part in, or maybe write a book. In other words, you should be closer to your audience, share as much as possible and it will be useful for your subscribers.

It is important to remember one thing: you are the one who brings all the sales. The more you write about what kind of person you are, what you like to do, about the innovations in your business, and what problems you face, how to solve them, or about the benefits of your product or service, the more trust your potential customers will have in you.

This may seem difficult for some people since it is necessary to carry out these activities on a regular basis, even though they don't bring instant monetary results.

Throughout 6 months, I was carrying out live streams, writing about my activity and the advantages of using my services, and talking about the consultations that I could offer. And I was almost ready to surrender, but then people began to write and send their requests to me. When I clarified how they learned about me, many said that they saw my live video and checked what I was writing. But it happened after 6 months. Perhaps you can get the result earlier. Especially when reading this book, since you already roughly understand what you need to do. I acted like a blind bat on Instagram, without understanding what actions need to be done first of all and relied only on my previous experience.

The most pleasant thing I can say in this chapter is that you cannot even imagine what a powerful machine it is to achieve your goals and gain potential clients.

Let me list the benefits:

First of all, you will start liking it, because you can always keep track of your chronology of events, so you can always compare yourself and your business on a yearly basis. Secondly, people will start contacting you to advertise their products/services in your account and they will pay money for that. Thirdly, having your own product (or service), you can always earn extra money, having at your disposal such a powerful resource as your Instagram account. You can even become an opinion leader and earn more on your Instagram account than on your product.

Below I want to describe how you can attract new subscribers to monetize your Instagram account and manage your popularity.

Selling through opinion leaders

Who are the opinion leaders and why is it worth selling through them? These are the people who have a large number of subscribers; therefore, they can influence large audiences and their opinion is more often heard. These can be popular bloggers. They can also help in the promotion of your account. It remains only to find them and agree on cooperation.

What can the opinion leaders give you?

Thanks to their opinion, your sales may skyrocket or the number of subscribers will rise sharply. How does it work? They can write a post about you, or feature in their stories and recommend you there. It is not very difficult to find an opinion leader and reach an agreement with them, but there are some pitfalls here. For example, there are a lot of fake accounts that take the money and disappear. Or the next problem is how to choose the right blogger so that they are as efficient as possible for you, what are the control points in choosing an effective opinion leader? And how to find one?

How to find an influential blogger?

• ask your friends, whom they have already worked with,

• find them using special software or website,

• contact an advertising agency that is dealing with such bloggers,

• find a telegram channel with reviews about working with certain bloggers.

You can check a blogger in the google search engine (or any other), just enter the account name or phone number of the one who offers you to collaborate and view reviews about this blogger.

What should I look for when analyzing a certain opinion leader?

122

- identify the number of interactions with this profile,

- find out the coverage (number of people who see publications),

- look at the audience (region, age, gender).

If everything looks great for you, then you need to find out the price and guarantees that this blogger will make a post or Stories about you.

After you have chosen a blogger by the above-mentioned criteria and ordered advertising, it would be great to analyze the quality of the work done. In order do this, create a link with a UTM tag (look in Google search), by which you can track the number of clicks on the link that the blogger has posted on his account.

I would advise you to avoid hiring an expensive blogger. Find bloggers who can advertise you for 10, 20 or 30 dollars. Write the text or script that this blogger will use or publish in their account. Make sure there is an appeal to visit your account or your website.

Think about what giveaway you can organize with this blogger. You can even offer a valuable prize or money.

Growing your audience through mass-liking and mass-following

This promotion method has been around since the creation of Instagram. Previously, it was possible to get a large number of subscribers and sales in a short period of time using this method. Everything depended only on which account to subscribe to and where your target audience is. Now, unfortunately, this method does not bring as many subscribers as we would like to, and also does not bring the number of sales that could have been expected earlier. And yet the method still works.

Some principles of how it works

There are so many services that allow you to do this. I will not describe a specific service, but I will describe the major work principle.

Define your TA

First, you need to define your target audience, assume which competitors may have it, and identify these indirect competitors.

Identify competitors

Indirect competitors are those who have a similar target audience that can spend the same money to buy goods or services that you offer. For example, if you have a premium-class beauty salon, then the premium-class spa salon will be your indirect competitor.

The next stage is gathering the audience of your potential customers. These may be the subscribers of your competitors, all those who like your competitors' posts or comment on them. I recommend taking as a basis all those subscribers who like and comment on the posts of your competitors because I believe that this is the most defined and active audience.

Don`t worry, you will not have to do it manually on your own, because all the difficult, time-consuming work will be done by special services you will be using. I will not recommend specific services, but you can always contact me at @Osetsimskiy and I will answer you.

Gathering an active audience

It is necessary to make active subscriptions, active likes and sending messages to competitive accounts, as well as to those who like and comment on competitive accounts. Of course, doing all this with the help of certain services.

How does it work?

When you subscribe to someone, they receive a notification and get curious and visit your profile. In case your profile attracts their attention, they would subscribe back to you. Same happens when you like someone's post or send a message.

That is why it is so important to shape up your profile because you will have exactly three seconds to interest your potential subscriber. If you have an incomprehensible avatar or weird profile name, most likely, they will not even check your profile.

Instagram limits

Of course, there are limits on Instagram. The maximum number of people you can subscribe to is 7500. Therefore, these services use unsubscribing. You do not need to worry about the fact that if you subscribe to 7500 people and then begin to unfollow, they will do the same. In fact, these subscribers would not understand that you have unfollowed them. It is important to program the auto-subscription service so that it would unsubscribe you first from those to whom you subscribed first.

So that you would not have the worry that the service will unfollow everyone and your friends, it provides two options - the white list and the blacklist. The white list does not allow unfollowing people to present in this list. The blacklist does the opposite.

Of course, there are also limits on subscriptions, likes, messages. These limits change every day. Non-compliance with these limits may result in blocking your account. In some services, these limits are provided immediately and do not allow the rules to be violated. And it is very convenient. If you are blocked for some reason, I recommend contacting an SMM specialist in order to avoid further harming your account and unlock it quickly.

How to get your account to the top in the search bar on Instagram?

At the moment, it really feels like a real war to become popular on Instagram. It is important to have the account in the top of the search list. The more often you get to the top, the wider the coverage is, and, as a result, the more subscribers can follow you.

So how do you get there?

In order to get to the top of the search on Instagram, it is necessary for your subscribers to make as many interactions with your posts and your profile as possible. First of all, it should be namely your subscribers. They should like, comment, save your posts, repost your posts and share them in their Stories, view your Stories, reply to them, write you in direct, view your live streams, and so on. And the more active your subscribers will be, the more likely you will get to the top of the search. However, besides this, it is important to regularly (and better constantly) get into the top of the hashtag search.

How to get to the top in the search by hashtags?

Under each post, you need to include from 5 to 30 hashtags. Since people subscribe to using them. I recommend doing the following - the first five hashtags should identify your occupation. It is also necessary to come up with such hashtags, according to which your potential client could find you.

Some principles of using hashtags:
• Use hashtags both in posts and in comments to your post. If you specify hashtags in the comments, you will still be found with these hashtags, while your text in the post will be more attractive.

• Use high-frequency hashtags (popular hashtags which have more than 1 million publications).

• Use low-frequency hashtags (hashtags up to a thousand publications). The more often you use different hashtags, the more unique your content would be valued by Instagram. The more unique your content is, the more chances you have to get to the top.

• Change the hashtags each time (this will increase your uniqueness).

• The more often you are at the top of the search by hashtags - the more subscribers you will get, as well as more chances to get to the top of the search.

There is a way that will allow you to get to be the top of the search by hashtags more often. Make your subscribers comment, like and save your posts.

How to get to the top of the hashtag search?

We specifically developed a certain service on Telegram. It's called FlyTOP. You will find a link at the end of the book. You need to follow this chat and everyone who is in this chat will subscribe to your Instagram account. Post links to your publications regularly and all the chat participants subscribe, like and comment on your posts. Moreover, they comment on exactly what you tell them. For example, you can tell them «Ask how much it costs».

Thus, you solve several problems at once. First of all, there is some activity under your posts (like if they want to buy something ») and potential clients would also start writing under your posts. According to statistics, it is difficult to get the first comment, and vice versa, as soon as comments have already been written under the post, people want to add their opinion too. The second problem, which is solved, is to get the top of the search.

Here is an example of using this method:

We tested this method using an account of our client who owns a yoga club. It took several days for the publications to hit the top by hashtags with the broad search request. At the moment, the yoga club is full of people! This is the result of 2 weeks only due to the hype created in the comments to the publications. Owners are already thinking about how to open more groups in the club.

Voilà my own example:

I have a lot of subscribers. I used the service for 2 weeks but could not get to the top through #marketing or # social networks hashtags and others. But I continued to actively ask to comment on my posts and ask to determine the prices. Two more weeks later two of my posts got to the top of the #socialnetwork hashtag search. This happened right during one of my workshops. I then took a selfie with all the participants on the background and asked everyone to leave me a comment, and in return, I would mention them in the post. Then I received 59 comments. Of course, this also influenced getting my post to the top.

I analyzed the statistics. Before getting to the top, my publications gained 300–400 likes, after I finally got to the top, I received 900 likes and 19 comments ONLY in 2 hours, while on the same day I received 2 orders to create a website! And the most surprising, after my publication was at the top, all the subsequent publications began to regularly hit the top too.

If your likes and comments or messages aren`t from your subscribers, then you just throw your money away. So, you do not earn. So, you are lagging behind trends and technologies. So, you lose money every day!

Thus, check THE NEXT conclusions about Instagram's algorithms:

- your posts should be liked and commented by your subscribers in order to be always in the top,
- to sell more, you need some "fake subscribers" who will be asking about the price and conditions under your selling posts,
- In order to be at the top of the search, it is necessary to increase the coverage of your publications.

You can start by having your friends comment and like your posts frequently.

Giveaways

Before you start using the Giveaway tool, you should understand what it is. Giveaway is by far the fastest way to get subscribers. But this does not mean that using only this method of attracting subscribers will contribute to skyrocketing your sales. There are pros and cons. Below, I will give a more detailed view of it.

How does Giveaway work?

The organizers create a contest account, offering various gifts for subscribers who have subscribed to all the sponsors (participants in the giveaway who, in return for a guaranteed number of subscribers, pay the organizers a contribution, which is later used to buy the gifts). The list of Sponsors can be found on the account where GiveAway is held. As a gift, they often offer a new iPhone or other gadgets.

Next, the organizers use various ways to advertise this giveaway account, including paid advertising, advertising through popular bloggers, or using own subscribers' audience. You should not be concerned about the ways they would use to achieve the popularity of the giveaway. It is important that they guarantee a certain number of subscribers. This may be 5000, 10000, or even 100000 subscribers over a certain period. This period can range from a week to two.

GiveAway types:

- personalized;
- thematic;
- universal;

Personalized Giveaway

In this case, the organizers find a famous blogger who has a large number of subscribers (usually over 200 thousand). Then, they create a backup account of this blogger, which the blogger refers to and tells their audience that certain gifts will be raffled among those who subscribe to all the sponsors. And all the subscribers of this blogger begin to subscribe to the sponsors, that is, those who paid for this giveaway and are included in the subscriptions list of the giveaway account.

The advantage of this method is that you can get the subscribers from this blogger. And this means that you can define the target audience, geolocation and other information that can be obtained from the statistics of this blogger.

Thematic Giveaways:

I believe that these are the best giveaways from the point of view of sales promotion since it is more likely to get an audience that is related to your product or service.

An online store of clothes, shoes, or cosmetics can be an organizer. Accordingly, gifts are goods from these stores. However, you can use both goods and services as gifts. For example, a spa session in a beauty salon, consulting, training.

My friend organized a thematic Giveaway for her target audience and she offered canvas, paints and all the things that an artist could need as a gift. Therefore, if you sell canvas, oil, paint,

such a Giveaway will be very useful for you.

Similar Giveaways can be carried out in real estate if the gift is a mortgage or a discount of 10% of the apartment price. If you are a realtor, the subscribers you will get through such a giveaway can play a key role. The disadvantage of such contests is a rather small number of subscribers.

Universal Giveaway:

This GiveAway is the easiest for the sponsors, as they allow you to attract the maximum number of subscribers.

How to organize it? When a regular account for GiveAway is created, this account gets advertised by a completely diverse audience. A large number of bloggers will take part, and all the subscribers who are attracted would be considered as a young audience. Their goal is to simply win a gift. Of course, they can remain with you after the giveaway ends, but you should not expect that they will buy something from you.

The disadvantage of such a giveaway is that the majority of those who subscribe to your account are freeloaders. That is, those subscribers who are not going to buy something from you in general, so the percentage of unfollows after the end of the giveaway will be high.

Pros and cons of GiveAways:

The advantage is that in a short period of time you get a large number of subscribers to your account. This influences the loyalty of potential customers: when they log into your profile, they see a large number of subscribers and understand that you can be trusted. This is the effect of hype.

For example, imagine that you go to a supermarket, and there a huge number of people are checking certain goods, talking to the cashiers. And imagine another situation when you are in a similar shop and there is emptiness there. As a rule, the credibility of such a store descends as there are many questions like the following «Maybe this product is of poor quality? » or «Maybe it is a shop with high prices? » And others.

The disadvantages of any of these giveaways are that in the end, you lose subscribers very quickly. The average percentage of unfollows is 40–60%. According to the Instagram rules, when there is a high activity of unsubscribing, it is suspected that you have a dubious account, and, as a result, your coverage and engagement get reduced. Consequently, this can adversely affect your sales, since your account will be shown less to potential customers. This can be tracked by the decreasing number of likes and comments. But, let's say, there is a trick that will allow you to avoid or minimize the risks of unsubscribing.

Before starting your Giveaway, it's important to:

• Prepare your personal profile. This means that all your photos must be processed through the same filter, and even better if they are in the same colour scheme. This will make your profile not look like a photo gallery.

• You need to develop posting strategies for the next month. This means that every day you should have at least 1 post, at least 3-5 Stories, and you should plan at least one live stream per week.

How to reduce the risks of unsubscribing:

• Agree with the organizer and carry out a live stream on the giveaway account.

• Prepare a list of topics that will be raised. It is necessary to communicate with the audience during your live stream with rhetorical questions. Ask questions which you are an expert in and answer these questions on your own. This will give the subscribers an understanding that you can be trusted. It is also worth declaring that you are going to carry out your own giveaway in your account after the end of this one. Thus, they will keep following your news.

• Prepare a giveaway that you will carry out in your account after the current one ends. You can use the simplest one, like giving away $50 prize using a raffle for those subscribers who would mention their friends in the comments under a certain post of yours.

- Plan a post where you would write what is your area of expertise and what you are going to do in this profile. For example, regularly holding Giveaways.

Agree with the organizer to hold a like-time on your five earlier posts, and in return, you will give someone $50 (the organizers will understand what you are talking about and will tell you how to do this).

After the like-time was carried out, you need to run targeted advertising using your expert post, which had been written earlier, to the audience that liked your posts over the last two weeks. Thus, you will remind them of your profile.

At the final stage, you need to start mass-liking and mass-following of the audience that communicated with your latest posts. Also, if you have something to sell, you can start automatically sending messages to the audience that interacted with your account during the participation in the GiveAway.

P2P. How does a personal brand affect sales?

It doesn't matter what you do and what you sell. The best way to get sales on Instagram is to sell it with a tool like a personal brand. B2B, B2C - are you serious? Nowadays people get attracted to people. In my practice, I faced the fact that many people don't know the name of my agency, but they know my name, many don't know what my agency does, but they know what I do.

I have a team of employees; there are sales managers, there is a person who is negotiating, but many clients want to communicate namely with me. At this point, I explain that my consultation will cost them 3 times more than the consultation of my project manager. And people want to pay more just to get me into their project.

Selling without a strong personal brand obviously means that it is impossible to get out of the rat race. A personal brand does not mean constant communication with the client. But this means that your work will cost much more.

The most important thing to understand is that the brand is not what you say about yourself or want people to say about you, but it is what people already think about you.

This is exactly the reason why before starting a business, I always ask myself two questions:

What do I need to do today to reach the expected result in half a year?

If I do it today, what will I reach in half a year?

Therefore, it is necessary to clearly know who are you, what are you doing, why are people contacting you, what is your personality. And you will see that your sales will increase.

How to create Insta brand?

It all begins with your target audience. You already know how to define it. In this subchapter, I would like to focus on making a brand of yourself, because 70% of success depends on how well your account is shaped up and how useful the content you post is.

Be sure to define your content strategy with the following:

- Articles
- Photo and video posts
- Stories

- Live streams

- Interviews

- Collaborations

Several promotion methods were explained in detail in the previous chapters, and I am going to target other methods below.

You need to remember one thing – you should write about yourself and how and who buys your product or service. The more you write simple, banal things, the more people will consider you an expert. If you would be writing many clever words, trying to show everyone that you are an expert, you will be less readable and it will be more difficult to reach the audience.

The basic principle of forming a personal brand is to show people what they already know to make them want to use your product. And that subsequently leads to a strong wish to buy

Let me give an example from the real estate field. To show your expertise, it is enough to tell people that a realtor is someone who is experienced, that when buying an apartment, you need to fill only two contracts. In fact, we give the clientt the information that they already know.

But having mentioned this information, the client who decides to buy an apartment will definitely contact this realtor, because they would have this strong assumption that namely, this realtor is a professional.

Consequently, by posting this information, the realtor brings the potential client this «I know that» feeling, and when offering the client a discount, they will want to receive this discount.

Stories

Stories are short videos with a length of 15 seconds. As you might have noticed, Instagram stories are popular. And indeed, it is so.

The world is overfilled with information; many simply get tired of tons of letters and texts. A lot of people write about the same thing using different phrases. And it can be annoying. Watching short videos is completely a different thing. In the video, you can share your energy, your emotions, while in two or three videos of 15 seconds you can tell everything that was supposed to be written in a long publication.

Based on my experience, I get the most of the sales through Stories. This happens because before watching a video it isn`t known what will be discussed in there unlike reading the publication where the subscriber immediately sees the entire text and can understand if it is a selling text or not. And if it is a selling text, they will most likely not read it.

Also, you should understand that at the moment there are already a lot of accounts on Instagram, and everyone is writing their posts, hoping that they will be read, and, therefore, your posts will not always be seen in the feed since it is too packed. While Stories are in priority, as they are always on top.

No matter what your business is, my personal recommendation is to make at least 3-5 stories per day. Thanks to this, your coverage and audience will be growing.

What to show in your Stories and how to use this feature?

- duplicate your posts in the Stories and add an appeal like "Check it out, folks"!

- make Boomerangs. You might have seen such videos that are repeated like on a constant loop. It's pretty simple: shoot something like birds flying away, cats walking down the street, or just yourself waving at your subscribers.

- Shoot a video of how you play sports, how you spend time at the beach. It is enough to take pictures of nature and not show your face, or even to say anything. Of course, if you will be talking, this will be more effective.

-    be sure to add emoji to the video,

-    add polls and other interesting widgets to your video, Instagram offers a large selection of them,

-    add links to each video,

-    write a few words on the video, mentioning, in brief, the key points of what you were saying in that video.

If you don`t have enough inspiration or don`t understand what to shoot, it is enough just to see what your competitors are sharing. Do not worry that someone will see something like this and will criticize you, as everyone is fixated only on themselves usually.

If you are still scared of sharing Stories - shoot at least something. Nobody will tell you that you are sharing nonsense, yet chances you will get additional orders are high!

Remember one thing: people watch videos more than reading posts. Only in 2017, video views increased by 80% compared with 2016.

IGTV

Relatively recently, Instagram has started offering the possibility to upload long videos. This feature is called IGTV. Currently, the maximum length of a video that can be uploaded is 10 minutes. And for the accounts with a large number of subscribers, it is 1 hour. In the future, it is planned to increase the maximum allowable length. The emergence of IGTV for bloggers means a new channel of monetization. Since they can advertise your business with this source and earn money.

Some experts consider that it is namely IGTV that will edge out YouTube because the video on Instagram does not require high quality (unlike YouTube). Many vloggers (video bloggers) go crazy with the acquisition of devices for shooting, processing and editing their videos and spend a lot of money on equipment, studio shooting, script. On Instagram, everything is simple, take your phone and make your videos.

Moreover, the IGTV channel provides an opportunity for viewing videos in the vertical position, and this cannot be done on YouTube.

Of course, I very much doubt that IGTV will crowd out YouTube, but it definitely brought the unique simplicity into the world of Vlogging!

I recommend you to already start uploading your videos on IGTV. If you don't understand yet what video to upload, post an interview, jokes, scenes from TV shows.

It will be great if you are already developing your video content for IGTV and will be spreading useful video content to your subscribers. No need to count on the fact that you can immediately receive a stream of clients from this source, but definitely it should be used!

Live streams on Instagram

On Instagram, as you know, it is possible to carry out a live stream.

What are they needed for?

In fact, I know they are very useful from different points of view:

- you liberate yourself, get rid of the fear of public speaking and opinion;

- you sell your services or products;

- you sell yourself as an expert.

I know from my own experience that people have a fear of going live and communicating with their audience. I will tell you my story about how I was afraid and then overcame my fear. One day my good friend, and co-author of this book, Alex Al-Vatar said: «I will help you!». I agreed and he developed a special strategy. At first, he offered to carry out a live stream for my subscribers together and share the time in this way: I will be speaking for 30% of the time, and he will be speaking for 70%. At the same time, Alex will ask some questions and communicate with my subscribers, and I will be just answering them, which was fine for me.

So, we went live. Alex began talking with my audience: he introduced himself and explained why we were going live and started asking me questions. I was not so scared.

For the second live stream, we agreed to divide the time by 50/50. This time I already was less scared than the first time. We went live, there was a lot of jokes from Alex, and I got that feeling of confidence.

The third lifestream was supposed to be a mirror image of the first - 70% of the time goes to me, and only 30% to Alex.

But! Before going live, he asked me:

Are you ready?

I am ready!

We were about to start, when he just hit the live button and said: "I need to use WC", took his bag and went out

And I'm left alone with my subscribers - it's like throwing a puppy into the water and let it swim out. And thanks to this experience, I gained maximum confidence.

Therefore, I recommend that you first carry out joint live streams with a more experienced person who has done that many times in the past. Plan a few topics for the live stream and start talking about everything you think, ask your subscribers a few questions, and answer their questions.

Here is an advice: Pre-write 10 questions you can answer during a random minute of silence.

Do not make a live stream last for more than 30 minutes. Write questions to be answered with your subscribers, like "How was it with you? Here is my experience".

It is very important to have live streams regularly. Create a schedule for yourself. For example every Tuesday at 12 pm or at 7 pm you do a live stream and communicate with your subscribers. Let it be 15-20 minutes, but regularly. Write a post - tell people that today at 7 pm you will be live to answer their questions.

Collaborations

Collaborations on Instagram are a process of joint actions of two or more people in order to achieve such goals as the exchange of subscribers (most often through joint live streams, recommendations in Stories, publications). It is very important to create collaborations with opinion leaders.

The advantage of these collaborations is that you will get new subscribers from the people who are interested namely in your account. In addition, the power of recommendations leads to a high purchase conversion rate.

In my work, I notice that when someone recommends me, I have to spend much less effort and energy to sell my services. In other words, the collaboration is when you are recommended or you recommend someone via Instagram or other types of social networks.

There are several types of collaborations:

1. Opinion leaders create posts about you, or feature you in their Stories, or tag you in a photo.
2. A blogger does a mutual promotion with you or like-time. The mutual promotion is a practice when a blogger recommends your profile to their subscribers, and you in return recommend their profile to your subscribers. This can be implemented as an exchange or for money. Like-time is when a blogger asks their subscribers to «Like» your posts.

3. You pay money to a blogger so that they will tag your account in their publication or in Stories.
4. You ask your client to write a review about your activity with a link to your profile.
5. Take a photo together and ask to be tagged in this photo.

I will now give an example of successful collaboration, and what I was doing for that:

I agreed with a blogger that we will make a joint live stream. This live stream consisted of two parts: during the first part, we will just be talking with this blogger in my account for 30 minutes on a specific subject and the blogger will talk about himself and his activity; and another 30 minutes, we communicate in the account of this blogger on my topics.

Such collaboration is difficult, but it is the most effective one. Thus, you get the maximum target audience.

Below you will find a step-by-step action plan:
- write a post in your account about the blogger you are going to collaborate with, and ask that blogger to do the

same for you. Notify your subscribers that your live stream will take place in the 3 days;

- the next day share the news about the upcoming lifestream in your Stories;

- on the third day, record a video for your Stories mentioning your live stream set to start tomorrow at a certain time and refer to the blogger's account (and ask the blogger to do the same for you);

- on the day of the live stream in your account, recommend that blogger to your subscribers, talking about his activity and usefulness. And ask the blogger to do the same for you;

- when you go live in the blogger's account, you need to tell the audience why they should subscribe to your account. In other words, you need to make an appeal for the action. For example, ask them to visit your profile and write comments under your post.

Scaling: How to win a new audience.

After you have determined your target audience, created your Instagram, developed a content plan, started using the above-described traffic options (advertising), you should think: what is the next thing to do? How can you influence and get more subscribers, more customers, and eventually, more sales?

Now you need to think about large-scale goals. I always ask myself what is the next thing. How else can I increase my popularity?

It all depends on your creativity and your type of activity. Here is an example of my plans:

- My personal public events and workshops.
- Taking part in certain events as an invited guest.
- Writing books.
- Participating in popular, well-known programs.
- Participating in TV shows.
- Getting featured on the radio talk shows.
- Participating in popular public projects.
- Participating in a charity project.
- Shooting in a movie.
- Writing articles about myself in popular magazines.

You can write a list of your own. And anything you participate in, you need to share your Instagram profile. And the bigger the list is, the bigger your result will be.

I have a good friend, whose debt is half a million dollars, and he continues to invest in his subscribers. Why do you think he is doing this? This is a rhetorical question. The more subscribers you have, the more influence you have. That is why Facebook bought the unprofitable WhatsApp messenger for $ 19 billion just because it had 600 million users.

It is important to set global goals for a year, for 3 years, for 5 years.

It is very difficult to understand what can be obtained through such an interval of time, especially being at the current level of thinking. After 5 years, you will be a completely different person, and your earnings may reach a completely different level. Often, setting the goals for a year, we overestimate ourselves but underestimate ourselves when we set the goals for the next 5 years.

Therefore, I use the following questions:

- How much do I want to earn?

- How many clients should I have?

- What processes must occur to get these clients?

- What team needs to be assembled to successfully complete all the processes?

Next, each process must be divided into subtasks, and for each subtask, you need to set own goals.

Thus, here is a practical task for you:

- Create an Instagram profile.

- Write a content plan.

- Take professional photos of your business.

- Find 5 opinion leaders and agree to collaborate with them.

- Take part in the available GiveAways.

- Plan to post Stories on a regular basis.

- Carry out 3 live streams and after each one write what was good and

    what didn`t work.

- Plan and create some collaborations with famous bloggers.

CHAPTER 4

CAPABILITIES OF TARGETED ADVERTISING
on Facebook and Instagram

Alexandr Kalinin

What is the targeted advertising? Let's define this concept.

According to Wikipedia, Targeting is an advertising mechanism that allows you to take under consideration only a part of the entire existing audience that corresponds to the specified criteria (target audience) and show your advertisement to this audience only.

How does targeted advertising work? When you create an account on social networks, you fill in a small form where you indicate your gender, age, place of residence, place of study, place of work, marital status, friends, participation in thematic groups, trips abroad. If we also add the fact that social networks track your behaviour and interests, then they receive a complete data package about you, which is available to an advertiser when setting up targeted advertising.

While setting up an advertising campaign, you can choose any combination of these data, which will allow you to target a very specific audience, for example it could be the residents of certain neighbourhoods, streets, people who have children, travellers, people interested in yoga, psychology, business, cooking, copywriting, development, Egyptian culture, basketball, vegetarianism, etc.

Believe me, all you can think of is already being used on Facebook.

For example, if you need to find housewives aged 30 to 35, who have children, like cooking, and at the same time have just returned from a trip 2 weeks ago, you will easily do it.

Just imagine what opportunities are opening up for you and your business if you can find an audience so easily. The main thing is to use these opportunities correctly. We will be analyzing all the features of Facebook and Instagram further on.

There is such information that you can rely on, and in this chapter, we will consider it point by point. And there is other information that the user fills in on their own. For example, «job». As a rule, people often do not indicate the actual state of things and are inclined to exaggerate. Therefore, it is impossible to completely trust such information. We'll have to check it. Apart from the major methods of determining the audience, there is still a large number of additional methods that we will discuss below.

Creating an advertising account

Imagine such a situation. You are considered a pilot, but you never learned to fly anywhere. You get into the flight deck and sit in the pilot's chair. You are excited. Even more, you really nervous, because you see a huge number of buttons, levers, light bulbs.

Then a flight attendant comes in and says that people are already boarding the plane. You feel frightened. How come? I don't know how to fly, I don't know the buttons, I don't even know where to start.

That is how I felt when I first looked at the advertising account on Facebook. You will feel the same. Then I made the biggest mistake because I decided to avoid checking these buttons. Today I regret that so much. I found an excuse for not doing this.

Only 2 years later I returned to the Facebook advertising account. I was very surprised because everything was actually so simple. I just had to wait a couple of days and let myself get used to it. Therefore, today I suggest that you, as a newbie pilot, but under my supervision, open your advertising account and push all the buttons you need to take off and then land the plane.

Yes, you can still learn how to do a dead loop, and fly on autopilot, and do different turns, but you will need another book for that.

Your advertising account

Imagine that you have a red Ford Mustang in your garage with a 5-litre engine and 700 horsepower. The maximum speed of this car is up to 320 km /h. And it accelerates up to 100 km /h in 3 seconds. If by chance you do not like this particular car, imagine your own version.

Do you know what is the saddest thing? That someone does not even know about the existence of this garage.

- Oh Really, do I have a garage? Does such a monster live there? I did not know!

But it is even worse when people know about the garage and about the supercar. But they lost the key to the car a long time ago and can`t make a duplicate.

And there is a third category of people who know about the garage, they go there to sit in their dream car every day. But they do not have gasoline to drive it.

So the garage with the car of your dreams is Facebook with its advertising account. Every Facebook's user already has it by default. Your responsibility is to use it correctly. It depends on you whether you will have a Mustang or an old broken car.

In this chapter, we will talk about the capabilities of your advertising account. Possibilities of advertising, which can work perfectly. Opportunities that you have already have, yet you probably did not know about them. I will teach you how to use them correctly and this will allow you to take your business to a whole new level.

Setting up your advertising account

Facebook is happy to give you the opportunity to spend money on advertising because this is one of the major ways Facebook can make money.

So the first thing Facebook will ask you to do is to attach a credit card to pay for your ads. To activate your credit card means to indicate its number, expiration date (month and year) and CVV-code (3 digits on the back of the card).

Just do it. Don`t worry. In my experience, and I have been working with advertising on social networks for more than 5 years and carried out more than 250 advertising campaigns, Facebook has never withdrawn extra money from my card without a reason.

Therefore, use your card safely. Any card of any bank will work. But it must support the Internet payment feature.

As soon as you activate the card, Facebook will withdraw $ 1 and immediately return it. So do not be alarmed, it is just checking your solvency (if you have money on the card). If you have the money, they can work with you!

The next thing to do is to choose the currency of your account. I also recommend you to have a credit card just for advertising on Facebook. It will allow you to control all the advertising costs.

What opportunities does advertising on Facebook and Instagram open for you?

We will be able to learn all the possibilities if we understand how the advertising account works and what tools are available for use.

So, how does Facebook advertising account work? Let's check it out. First of all, let us understand that the creation of an advertising campaign consists of three stages.

The first stage is the creation of the campaign itself. The main task of this stage is to determine the correct objective. To do this, you need to determine what do you want to receive from the advertising on Facebook (subscribers, applications, video views, coverage). You can create an unlimited number of advertising campaigns and set a different objective for each of them.

The second stage is the creation of ad groups. Who and where will we advertise? At this stage, we choose the audience, the place and schedule of showing the ads, set the budget. The number of ad groups is unlimited within one campaign.

At the third stage, our task is to create the advertisement itself. In one group there can be up to 6 advertisements. Later, we will analyze each stage and determine the opportunities namely for your business.

Choosing the main objective for your advertising campaign

There are 11 advertising objectives on Facebook. Let's gloss over each of them and choose our own objective that is as appropriate as possible for your business. Each objective includes its own algorithm on Facebook. Let's imagine that 11 objectives in your advertising account are like 11 members of a football team. The common task of all the players is to win the match. Score an objective more than the opponent. But each player on the field has own personal task/objective:

- the objective of the keeper - to catch the ball,
- the defender - to seize the ball from the opponent and do not let the opponent score,
- the forward - to score a goal.

Do you agree? Ok, but the defender can score too, although this is not their main task. This will be just a nice bonus for the team.

This is very similar to the objectives of the advertising account. The overall mission of all the objectives in the advertising account is to help you get more audience, more requests, and increase brand awareness. At the same time, each objective has its task, which it can do the best.

Let's determine the tasks of each objective.

The «Brand awareness» objective: How to increase your brand's awareness of the ess?

The Facebook algorithm will choose to show your ad to the people who are most likely to remember it and your brand.

Unfortunately, this objective is not for everyone. I have tested it many times and I will tell you honestly that I have mixed feelings because it is rather difficult to evaluate the results of its use on practice. After all, there are no indicators that will make it clear whether people have really memorized the advertised brand, as we can't track their reaction. For this reason, I rarely use this objective.

The «Reach» objective. How to show ads to the maximum number of people?

This objective allows you to show your Facebook ads to the maximum number of people. This objective does not require any specific actions from people, so it will not be suitable for promoting specific goods or services. But it will work perfectly if you need to get some quick coverage of wider audiences. That is why I see the purpose of this objective exclusively for the rapid spreading of news. If you are dealing with just this task, then choose this objective. However, I will further analyze the objectives that you will be more likely to use.

The «Traffic» objective. How to get more links to the site?

Imagine such a situation. It`s at 5 am. You are fishing. It is still dark, but you will see the sun going up soon.

It is calm. The float is perfectly visible. In a minute, you pull out a 2-pound fish. Then throw it over again and pull out another fish, exactly of the same size. Then again and again. And always the same fish. And you keep getting them all day long. You are approached by other fishermen. People gather around you. They ask «How do you do this?» You kindly grin, because you feel great. And you decide to share the secret. It is simple: everyone uses a usual worm, and you have an unusual. It`s is able to attract the fish. It goes into the water, and calls certain fish, not allowing the other ones to approach.

This is how Facebook optimizes your advertising depending on the objective you have chosen. When choosing the «traffic» objective, it will show your ads only to those people who are most likely to go to the website. Not those who will just like the advertising post, and not those who will comment on it, but those who will click on the link in the post. We often use this objective to advertise online stores. When you need to sell your goods, we offer to learn about their characteristics in the online store, and carefully leave a link to go to it.

Therefore, if you have an online store or a website on which your products are presented, choose the «traffic» objective and get a lot of visits from the users of social networks - Facebook and Instagram.

The «Engagement» objective. How to make people comment on your posts?

An ad that aims to increase involvement is designed to encourage people to check your post, leave a comment or like it. The main task is to induce a person to start interacting with your post. What is involvement? It includes comments, reposts, likes, replies to invitations, acceptance of offers. You may have already encountered the «Engagement» objective when Facebook offered you to «raise the publication» on your business page.

For whom and in what cases will this objective be the most useful?

In those cases, if you have an interesting post on the page and you want to increase the coverage for it (to attract as many people as possible) or you want to promote your services or educational projects, then when choosing this objective, people will be able to join you even by commenting on the post.

For example, using this objective, we successfully invite teens to join psychological workshops. How does it work?

First of all, we write a post on the business page on Facebook saying we are going to hold a workshop for pre-teenagers from 9 to 11 years old very soon. Later we explain the reasons why it is necessary to take part in the workshop. And share the workshop program itself. This text is intended for parents, or rather, for mothers. After all, namely they make the decision about the participation of their children in such an event.

Next, we choose the «Engagement» objective. By launching the advertising featuring this objective, Facebook algorithms will find people who are more likely to get involved and will be joining the workshop in the post. This is exactly what we need for the moms to register their children for the training in the comments. It worked great for us. Only using this objective, we gather groups for workshops every month.

The «Installing applications» objective. How to get a lot of mobile app installations?

This objective allows you to increase the number of installations of your mobile application. If you have a mobile application that you have developed, and you want to increase the number of users, then, by setting up an advertisement, choose this objective. Facebook will show the ads to those people who are most likely to click on your ad and download the application.

Let's analyze an example.

You have created your own personal mobile app for iPhone, which counts calories and helps you to find out what and how much you need to eat to keep fit. And you decided that such an application would be useful not only for you but also for all the people who want to lose weight. You have recommended the application to your friends, everyone liked it and kept spreading the word about it among their friends. This has made you even more pleased, and you want the whole world to know about your super-useful application. You go to Facebook and start advertising, using the «Installing the application» objective and the ads are shown to those who would be willing to install this useful application on their phone. That's how simple it is. And there are no pitfalls.

The «Video views» objective. How to show videos to those who will watch them?

Using this objective, Facebook will show your videos to people who are most likely to watch them. You can use that objective to promote the videos that show what happens behind the scenes, product reviews, customer stories, useful thematic videos.

For example, I use the «Video views» objective to promote useful videos, as well as for promoting live streams, which I carried out on my business page. By doing so, I cover more and more people.

When choosing the «Video views» objective there are two main benefits:

you increase the outreach of people who get to know you from your videos

Facebook offers the opportunity to choose a separate audience of people who have already watched your videos and target them with your ads. And this, as you already understand, is a warm audience. Later, we will discuss how to create an audience in detail.

The «Lead Generation» objective. How to receive orders from potential customers?

This is one of the most important objectives. With its help, you will show your ads to those people who are most likely to leave a request and indicate their phone and e-mail.

Facebook tools allow you to create an advertising campaign and registration form. Thus, when a user sees your advertising post and gets interested in your offer, they can click the «find out more» button and send a request for a service or product directly on Facebook.

This objective is ideal for signing people up for events, such as courses, workshops, seminars, webinars, master classes. That is when you need to get a customer's phone number. And then call them, invite to come to the event and pay for it there. It works great for selling any services when you offer consultations, and during the consultation, you offer the client to order your service or buy goods.

The «Engagement - Messages» objective. How to receive messages from potential customers?

With this objective, you can increase the number of people chatting with your company on Facebook Messenger. This will allow you to finalize purchases, answer questions, provide support.

We use this objective very often in promoting educational products and selling services.

When people see your advertisement, they have the opportunity to click a button and contact you in Messenger. Thus, you involve them in correspondence, where you can already tell more about your services or offer to sign up for events.

There is another feature of this objective. If you connect a chatbot to your page, you can memorize and collect all the people who wrote you in Messenger. Within the book, we will not discuss how chatbots work, but you should be aware of them because they open up great opportunities for your business.

The «Conversion» objective.

This objective is very similar to «Lead generation».The main difference is that with this objective you lead people to the site. And at the same time, you choose what Facebook will be considered as a conversion.

In essence, the conversion is a kind of targeted action. For example, with the help of this objective, we are promoting our master classes in different cities. As a conversion, I can choose «Sign up on the site» and it turns out that Facebook will be looking for people who are most likely to register on the site.

Can you imagine the possibilities of advertising? Facebook itself is looking for people for me who are ready to register on the site and will be trying to show ads only to these people.

How does it work? For example, Mary went to the site, read the information about a product, looked at the reviews, and didn`t leave a request. And then Mike visited the site and left a request. Then everything happens like in a movie about FBI agents: the profile of each user who visited the site gets analyzed.

Mary: 32 years.

Interests: English, children, cooking.

Region: Kiev region.

Behaviour: travels frequently.

Mike: 30 years.

Interests: business, extreme sports.

Region: Lvov region.

Behaviour: active buyer.

And there are a lot of such criteria for analysis. And only after this, Facebook decides that it will not show ads to Mary and people like her anymore, but will try to show them more to people who have the same interests as Mike`s.

The «Product catalogue sales » objective. How to sell products through an online store on Facebook?

With this objective, you can create advertisements that automatically display products from a catalogue that best fit your target audience. I practically do not use this objective. There are much simpler ways to sell products through an online store on Facebook.

The «Store Visits» objective. How to attract people to your offline store?

With this objective, you can attract people to your offline stores. It allows you to promote several locations at once among the people residing nearby. Facebook uses geo-targeting based on radius and other unique advertising features (for example, the native store locator). Taking it simply, it is when you advertise to those people who are close to your store or salon and invite them to come in. It`s perfect!

Therefore, we discussed all the major objectives of an advertising campaign. Now your task is to choose an objective that will maximally meet the requirements of your business.

Facebook audiences

How to find people to show them your ads? How to advertise to the target audience?

As I already said, there are so many ways to get an audience on Facebook even before setting up an advertising campaign. Let's check them. So what opportunities does

Facebook offer us? They name it an «individualized audience» or a «customer database».

Most likely, you already have a database of clients you work with. And you know their emails or phone numbers. Perhaps you also have a subscriber database and these are the people who have subscribed to your business pages on Facebook and Instagram.

The point is that you can use this. All you need is to transfer this database to Facebook and create an audience from it. Admit it, this is a perfect and warm audience to offer products or services to.

In order to do that you need to:
• create a standard file in Notepad (with the .txt extension) or Excel table, where you can indicate the phone numbers or e-mails of your customers;
• upload this file to Facebook.

That`s all. Then Facebook will do everything for you. It will try to find these people - after all, as you remember, we register on Facebook by mail or phone number - and create the audience.

How can this audience be used?

Have you ever noticed how large companies work? For example, BMW.

Three years ago I went for a test drive of a BMW X5. After that, every six months, I was regularly receiving calls from them asking me if I made up my mind to buy a car.

And this is a very powerful marketing ploy. This is how BMW uses its database of people who did not buy anything from them but had a test drive.

I am sure that for those who have already bought a car, there are the same calls, only with other questions and offers. Imagine, how you can use this in your business. What can you offer your customers right now? What products or services can they still order?

For example, I have the extra-sales, this is the main source of profit. After all, it is much easier than constantly looking for new customers. If a client has ordered an advertising campaign on Facebook and Instagram, then I will definitely offer to design a website and advertising on Google a bit later, or maybe installing a CAM system (customer accounting system).

And what can you offer to people who have not bought anything from you? And to Your Subscribers? After all, if they somehow came to you, it means they had an interest in your products or services. Offer your goods to these people.

The «People who have visited your site» audience

If you have a website, then you probably noticed that not all the people who visit it, leave their requests or buy something. I will even say more: people who want to buy something from the site account for only 1-3% of the total audience.

It turns out that only 3 people out of 100 will leave you their contacts. And the remaining 97 people? They will just pass by, and this is unacceptable! After all, as a rule, we have to spend money to attract people to the site.

Why does it happen? Everything is very simple. The fact that so many people pass by does not mean that they accidentally hit the site or they are not interested in your products. Most of them just take a pause to think, to look at similar products from competitors, someone is waiting to get the salary, someone was not in a comfortable position to check the site at work and they will return later. And there are a lot of such reasons.

Therefore, our task is to return these people to the site.

Do you know how smart people work on Facebook? They have already thought about everything. We are offered to solve our problems through a small «code», which is called «Pixel Facebook».

It can be copied from your Facebook advertising account. In order for a pixel to start working, it must be embedded in the code of your site. This will be enough for it to memorize all the people who came to the site, and moreover, those who were on the site but did not order anything.

In addition to analyzing the work of the site and studying the behaviour of its visitors, the obtained data is used to configure the so-called «retargeting» (or «remarketing»). Or, call it simply – a sort of a catch-up game. I am sure you have already seen such an advertisement. Most often it is used by the companies selling equipment, as well as any other online stores.

Let's give an example of this type of advertising. Imagine, you have an online store selling women's dresses. A

27-year-old lady came to the site and checked a «red evening dress». However, She did not buy it and closed the site.

So, you can easily track it and adjust advertising with this dress to target this girl, for example, on Instagram. You can offer to buy a dress right now and get it with a 10% discount and free shipping.

It is unlikely that she will refuse. According to statistics, you can return up to 30% of those who left the site and sell them your products.

This advertisement works very well when you have cyclical sales. What does it mean? For example, you sell diapers and you know that a large package is enough for a week. So a week after the purchase, you can target your customers with this advertising and offer them to buy diapers «because they will soon run out of them" and offer the door-to-door delivery option.

Well, in general, you understand that «traffic from the site» audience is also a warm audience that already knows you, is familiar with the products, saw your offer on the site. And this should be used!

The «People who installed your mobile app» audience

We analyzed the objective of "Install apps" advertising campaign. So now we can create an audience that was interested in your mobile application.

Let's check an example. Do you remember our mobile calorie counting app we promoted in the «Installing the application» objective? So now we can have the list of people who installed the application. Moreover, we can create a list of people who not only installed the application but who live in Kiev or are more than 30 years old.

Why do you need this audience? This is already a warm audience that has seen and used your application. Offer them other products made by your company.

The «People who interacted with you on Facebook and Instagram» audience

The next audience includes several audiences:

People who watched your videos:

You can create an audience that watched your videos. Select the viewing time: from 3 seconds to full viewing. It is clear that the videos can be of different length. I have live streams on Facebook that last 90 minutes. In this case, it would be wrong for me to take an audience that saw it entirely. 10–25% will be enough and this will give me an understanding that people were interested in my video.

On the other hand, there are videos lasting up to 60 seconds, in this case, a much higher percentage will watch it to the end. But even watching a 10-second video gives an understanding of whether people are interested or not. I regularly gather an audience of people who watch my videos. This is a very nice warm audience who knows who I am. They can be offered different products and training.

People who filled in the «Lead Generation Form»

Do you remember, we discussed the concept of «Lead Generation» objective? So, now we have an opportunity to gather all the people who not only left the applications but also opened the registration form.

This gives us another warm audience, which can be offered various product variations.

People who have been on your Facebook business page. .

You can create an audience from the subscribers to your business page. You can select everyone who interacted with your business page publications. If you already have such an audience, you can safely start advertising targeting it.

But here, it is important to understand that in case the audience on your business page is not a target one, but consists of your friends or acquaintances who you have invited to like your page so that the page does not look empty, then you should not target this audience. Return to this later when the business page gains an organic warm audience.

People who have checked your Instagram business profile.

If you already have a business profile on Instagram, then you can also gather an audience that has already interacted with your posts: gather all the people who liked, commented, or viewed your posts. It will also be a very warm audience.

People who considered or wanted to come to your event

As you already know, you can create events on Facebook. Accordingly, you can gather an audience that somehow reacted to this event: people who were going to come or answered that they would think about joining it.

Similar audience

Imagine that you have a database of 300 phone numbers of your customers. You upload this list to Facebook. Facebook offers you: «Let us find you a similar audience. We will analyze all your clients and determine their age, gender, interests, behaviour on social networks and find another 100,000 to 1 million similar people». Believe me, Facebook can do it very well. Be sure to create a similar audience.

You can also create a similar audience from the people similar to those who watched your videos, or those who visited your site or interacted with your business page or Instagram account.

Standard audience settings. How to choose the region, gender, and age of the target audience?

We have examined the ways to create «individualized audiences» that allow you, even before the start of an advertising campaign, to find your warm audience who can be offered to buy something. But there are cases when you do not have a single «individualized audience». Perhaps you are just starting your business. Therefore, now we will consider the standard audience settings that will allow you to find your target audience on Facebook and Instagram.

Demographic Data

Region:

Select the region where your target audience, who you want to show the ads, should be located. You can advertise to the entire world, but you can also choose a small region. If you have, for example, a local business, you can choose an audience that is located near your business.

Age:

You can choose the age of the target audience, which varies in the settings from 18 to 65 years. Be careful with this setting. At this stage, despite its simplicity, a lot of mistakes are made. As a rule, all entrepreneurs believe that absolutely all people from 18 to 65+ can buy their products. I am sorry to upset you, but it is not true. More precisely, this may be so, but there is a more specific audience that does this much more often than the rest. Therefore, it is important to divide the audience, as people of different ages make different purchasing decisions. A girl of 18 years and a man of 55 years old will definitely use different criteria.

Gender

It is possible to choose the gender. You can advertise to either men or women or both.

Languages

You can choose the language your audience speaks. This audience setting means your Facebook language. I do not always use these settings.

Detailed targeting

Interests. You can choose the interests of those people who you want your ads to be showed to. What does it mean?

Facebook knows what is interesting for us because every day you somehow show yourself: you comment on some posts, like and watch videos, communicate in some groups. Based on this data, Facebook assigns your specific interests. Now imagine that you are selling sports nutrition, and you need to find people who are engaged in sports. What are the interests of these people? That's right, it is a sport. This may be fitness, football, gym, etc.

In addition to interests, it is possible to find a target audience using other indicators:

- Behaviour.
- Job
- Employers.
- Education.
- Life Events.
- Family status.
- Industry.

Using this tool only you can find the audience you need. For example, you offer yoga classes. What are the interests of people on Facebook and Instagram who are interested in yoga? Are these people interested in sports? Yoga? Stretching? Eastern culture? Spiritual Development? Yes, of course!

Or maybe you sell evening dresses for girls. What interests can these girls have? They go to clubs, theatres, they love shopping. And can girls interested in sports, fitness buy dresses? Yes, of course, they can. It turns out that you can also target them in your offer to sell evening dresses, shopping it up in such a way: «Evening dresses perfect for active girls». We will talk later how to analyze and segment an audience. And now think what are the interests of your target audience? Write out all the interests and do not discard anything yet.

Placement. Where will my ads appear?

Placement is a place where your advertisements will be shown.

Below you will see a complete list of places to show your ads

> **on Facebook:**

- Instant Articles
- Videos
- Featured Videos
- Marketplace
- Stories

> **Instagram**

- Feed
- Instagram Stories
- Audience Network
- Native ads, banners, and inserts
- Bonus Videos

➤ Messenger

- Home page
- Advertising messages

By default, Facebook offers you do not edit the list of placements, but leave it as it is. But I recommend that you first do not include all the types of placement, and leave only those that we will consider below.

We will not analyze all the placements, but only those that can be used more effectively in your business. I still advise you to try to place your ads everywhere so you can understand which place is more effective namely in your case. I always use Facebook and Instagram feeds because they make up the most versatile and spacious place to run ads that will suit most advertisers.

Check the right column. This is the text that you can see only from your PC. Check your Facebook page and you will see different advertisements on the right side. And pay attention to the fact that when you are listing your feed, the right column stays there, it is always on top and always seen.

We frequently use it when we want people to remember about us. For example, when we advertise an event, we can show the date of this even right in this section on the right side.

Placement in Stories

Stories are shown both on Instagram and Facebook. This is a very effective place if used correctly. Advertising here is very cheap: $ 0.02. You can get transitions to the site for only 2 cents. Be sure to try to start advertising here. Important features of this placement are that the photos should be prepared in advance. First of all, the photos should be vertical and quadrangular (as if you are making pics using your phone). Secondly, it would be better to write a text on the photo, and it can be an appeal for action (click on the link to the site or write a Message).

Messenger.

You can show your ads where you chat with your friends. Very often, people are in this very place and there will be no longer any distracting factors. Only your advertisement. Try it.

The design of your ads. How will your advertisement look like?

On Facebook and Instagram, you can choose the design of your advertisements:

- In-image advertising
- Video advertising
- Facebook Carousel Ads
- Banner advertising
- Slideshow Advertising
- Canvas ad cover image

Most often we use In-image advertising. This format is the easiest to create: you just need a picture for advertising. Facebook has even thought about this, so in the advertising account, it offers you a large stock of cool photos that you can use for your advertisements absolutely free. There are a lot of photos covering any subject.

The ads with images, either photos or graphics will suit any kind of business, since with the help of a picture you can always show your product, service or event.

In order for the pictures to work even more effectively, I recommend adding a text over them. But make sure the text doesn't cover more than 20% of the image. Facebook offers a specialized tool to check the images before publishing the advertisement -

https://www.facebook.com/ads/tools/text_overlay

Video Advertisements

This is one of the most effective types of advertisements at the present moment. If you have a high-quality promotional video, you definitely need to create an advertising campaign featuring this video. I am sure, the advertising payout would be much higher in this case compared to in-image ads.

We are using video ads for almost any business. You can record a video invitation to join your master class, carry out a lifestream and share a story about your products and services, you can record a video and invite people to get a counselling session with you, or show the behind-the-scenes (for example, how your product is manufactured) and many other things. Experiment with various videos and use them in your advertising campaigns.

Slide show and Carousel Ads

We often use slide shows and carousels in the design of our online-stores, since this gives us a great opportunity to show many products from the assortment at once.

I have a client who designs clothes for pregnant women. She uses only slideshows and advertisements on Instagram. Her slideshow consists of 10 photos, showing 3 products, like 3 different photos per product. And this works just wonderful for her business.

Advertising budget. How much do you need to spend on advertising?

How to choose a budget for advertising?

If you are just starting to work with advertising on Facebook and Instagram, there is no need to use huge advertising budgets. Even, on the contrary, you need to run your first campaign with a minimal budget. So you definitely will not spend a lot of your own money on advertising (which might be spent in vain), but gain the necessary experience.

With that being said, I recommend using a maximum of 3-5$ as a daily budget. This will be enough to reach 400–1000 users per day and get some results.

The minimum advertising term is at least one day. But in 1 day you will most likely not understand what happened. This is a too short period of time. Facebook needs more time to find the audience you need and optimize your advertising. Therefore, your advertising should work for at least 3 days. And the more, the better.

What are you paying for when using Facebook advertising?

Remember, as this is important! We pay for our advertising getting showed to people. We pay to reach our target audience.

Let's take an example, we helped an online children's clothing store and we spent $ 10 on 3-day advertising. With this money, we received coverage of 1000 people. This means that 1000 people saw our ads. From this 1000, 100 people clicked on a link in the ads, and they went to the website. It turns out that for $ 10 we received 100 transitions to the site (clicks). Accordingly, one click cost us $ 0.1.

Let's take another example. We still have the same children's clothing online store and we spent $ 10 again on advertising for 3 days. With this money we received the coverage of 1,000 people, that is, 1,000 people saw our ad. And from this 1000 nobody clicked on the link in our ad. So, for $ 10, we received 0 clicks to the site, which means we just spent $ 10. As you can see, in any case, regardless of the outcome, Facebook takes money only for reaching people. Therefore, our task is to set up an advertising campaign and select the target audience so that for these $ 10 as many people as possible interact with our ad: click on the link, write a comment, leave a request, write in Messenger, etc.

The most frequently asked question from entrepreneurs is «I tried to run ads and it does not work. Why?»

And here, unfortunately, there are so many reasons. We have just discussed one of them. Your ad design is trivial, not attractive and not interesting for people to even check.

The next reason is that your offer itself is not interesting to people. You may have a chic, attractive design, and an offer that does not make anyone want to know more about it.

In addition, you might be not able to choose the right target audience. You have a wonderful design and the offer is excellent, but you show your advertising to the wrong people, not of that age, not in that region.

You can just disable your ads before your customers see it. It happens often. Beginners start advertising and turn it off in one day, spending $ 3. Unfortunately, you will not be able to understand how effectively the advertising campaign worked in such a short period of time.

Next, we will pay attention to writing advertising texts, and also talk about how to make your advertising get more attention.

Assessing the efficiency of the advertising campaign

Have you ever placed an advertisement on a billboard? Or maybe you ordered the flyers that were distributed on the street? And have you always been able to track the results of these advertising campaigns?

Most entrepreneurs who pay money for placing a billboard do not know how effective this advertising has worked. How many people saw the billboard? How many of them called? How many made an order? It turns out, no one knows whether the cost of advertising has paid off.

The situation is completely different when it comes to Facebook. You have complete and detailed statistics at your disposal. You can find out the exact number of people who saw your ad, as well as how many of them made an order or clicked on it. Moreover, you will immediately find these people in the social network.

Unlike other ads, advertising on social networks gives you a very fast way to reach the potential audience and choose the exact audience that you need! We will talk more about the analytics and improving advertising campaigns in the next subchapter.

3 ways to set up Facebook and Instagram ads

I am sure you can't wait to launch an ad campaign. I will help and share the 3 ways to do it.

Each method has several pros and cons. Let's talk about each of them.

Learning how to set up the advertising on your own:

Pros:

- You will learn how to set up your ads on your own.
- You will understand how advertising account works.

- You will learn how to write marketer texts for advertising.

- You will understand how to choose images for your ads.

- You will be able to further customize ads for any of your projects.

- You can help friends and customers.

- You will find out what result you can get with the help of advertising; it will be easier to delegate this task in the future.

Cons:

If you are new in this business, you will need diligence and patience, as you will need a lot of time to get used to the interface of the advertising account and understand all its functions and buttons.

It takes some time. If you are an entrepreneur, I am sure you still have many other responsibilities.

There is a chance to make a mistake in the settings and spend money in vain.

As you can see, there is a number of advantages and some disadvantages. My advice to you is to learn how to set up the ad campaigns on your own because it is not as difficult as you think. And most importantly, you know your target audience better than anyone else, you know your customers. After all, you communicate with them every day, you know their problems, pains. And when you understand how to work and what results to expect from advertising, you can easily delegate it.

Finding a freelancer:

Pros:

• For a relatively small payment, you can order the setting up of your

advertising campaign.

• It is not necessary to understand how advertising works.

Cons:

• It is hard to find a good specialist, as high-qualified professionals are

usually busy.

• You can't be confident that they will do everything to the highest

quality standards.

• You can't determine if that specialist is competent in this field.

As you can see, this option has more cons than pros. But I do not want you to think that all freelancers will not work well. Although in most cases this is what happens. I have to warn you about this.

But if you managed to find a good specialist - keep them! You probably saw a lot of similar headlines in advertising: «How advertising made a person rich in one day», «How he managed to sell 300 products in just 2 hours» or «How to get 100 sales every day».

On the Internet, there is a huge number of such tales. And you start asking yourself - How do they do it? What am I doing wrong? Where can I find a specialist who can exactly do the same for me?

I want to share with you some information regarding what can be true out of all that and where are deceived, and they are not sharing the entire story.

Let me say success stories happen, and such cases probably exist. I use "probably" here because I cannot answer for all the dishonest specialists. And such niches where you can quickly make a huge amount of orders also exist, although there are not so many of them.

I didn't believe it exactly until I myself had such a story. We made an advertising campaign for a travel agency, named «Getting Visas to Poland». One hour after the launch of the advertising campaign, the client called and asked to turn off the advertising campaign. There have been so many calls that he did not even have time to prepare. He said that while he was talking to a potential client, there were 2-3 unanswered calls. He then switched on the advertisements every day for just 60 minutes.

There was another advertising campaign for a car service station that offered to install gas equipment on the vehicles. The result was exactly the same. There was a flurry of calls. The customer opened 4 more stations in 2 other cities in 2 months.

But remember! You should not be misled by these niches. For each of these examples, all advertising campaigns were launched at the right time.

For «Getting Visas to Poland» it was a very busy period since it was at that time that the war began in Ukraine. And people were looking for options to protect themselves and started getting visas to Poland.

Converting a car to LPG was also a very relevant service. At that time, the price of petrol jumped to an unrealistic height, and in comparison, gas was very cheap.

But in most cases, advertising campaigns on social networks regularly bring customers. As a rule, there are no such bright bursts, no millions earned in one day. But they work and bring several new customers every day.

For example, we had a client who worked with us for one year. When he first contacted us, he owned only one beauty salon for men, called «Barbershop», and a year later he was already about to open the 4th, which is currently the largest one in Ukraine. Advertising played an important role in the development of his business since it was bringing new customers every day on a regular basis.

Therefore, first of all, it would be good to know what results the freelancer already has. And if they have any experience in your niche. It would be perfect if the person had experience setting up advertisements in your field of activity, and already understands how to reach your target audience and, most importantly, already had some kind of results.

Contacting an online marketing agency:

Pros:

• Online marketing agencies, as a rule, employ good specialists.

• You can sign an agreement.

You can be sure they will not vanish anywhere after getting your payment.

Cons:

• A good agency will ask a high price for the service.

• No mobility in decision making.

• They do not provide details of the fulfilled advertising campaigns.

I am often approached by entrepreneurs who ordered advertising campaigns in agencies, but they are not satisfied with the results. And they would like me to improve their advertising campaign. But it turns out that advertising campaigns stats remain at the agency, and those entrepreneurs do not have any access to that data.

If you stop working with the agency, then you have nothing left. Even though you paid money for setting up an advertising campaign. Not all agencies work like this. Therefore, before signing the contract, be sure to find out all the details.

There is one important thing in working with an online marketing agency. Many agencies take a share of your advertising budget.

This is convenient if your advertising budget starts from $ 10,000 per month. Then the agency services will cost you only $ 1000 (10%). But if you have a small budget, say $ 100–300 per month, then I doubt you will find an agency that agrees to work with you for $ 10.

But here it is important to understand one vital thing. If you have a tested plan and you have already launched it into an advertisement and got the first result, and now it is important for you to only get more traffic, then this is the case when you can go to the agency.

In the next chapter, we will explain how to effectively manage an advertising campaign, how to spend less on advertising and attract more customers or how to optimize your advertising. We will also analyze the concept of the target audience which includes such points as who and where we sell, and how to analyze your competitors.

Here is a practical task for you:

- Add a credit card to pay for advertising on Facebook.
- Upload the customer database and create your «Customer database» audience.
- Create a «People who have been on your business profile» audience
- Create «People who interacted with your business page» audience.
- Create a «People who watched your videos» audience.
- Create a «People who interacted with your Instagram business account»
    audience.
- Determine the placement strategy.
- Choose the design and format of your ads and gather materials for advertising.
- Create a «People who visited the event» audience.
- Create a "People who filled in the «Lead Generation Form» audience.

Chapter 5

HOW TO EFFECTIVELY MANAGE AN ADVERTISING CAMPAIGN

Alexandr Kalinin

First of all, you need to know a few important nuances that affect the results in order to manage your advertising campaign effectively.

Facebook provides opportunities for all businesses. Your task is just to choose the right tool.

Effective ad campaign management means that you:

- know your target audience very well and understand its desires and problems;
- understand how to use this knowledge in an advertising campaign,
- know how to segment an audience;
- know your competitors
- can analyze and optimize advertising campaigns to get better results.

We will analyze all these points in this last chapter of the book.

Your Target Audience

A target audience is a group of users which certain promotional activities are directed on, which the advertisers are interested in and which is interested in certain information.

Customers whom we can sell

What kind of people are they? Where do they live? If you work in the B2B segment, who would make the decisions? What is the general portrait of these people? Is it possible to designate their average age? Are they men or women? How their day goes? What do they do? Do they have problems that prevent them from living in peace? What are they dreaming about? What do they madly want?

It is very important to know the answers to these questions. And it would be better if you would not answer these questions on your own, inventing answers out of your head. It would be much better to ask your clients and subscribers to answer these questions.

But if you have no customers, what should you do then? There are two ways to answer all these questions.

The first way is to do it yourself, thus simply assuming.

We «assume» that our target audience lives in Kiev, Ukraine. These are women from 30 to 40 years old, they have children, etc. But is it really so? This will have to be tested in reality by launching an advertisement targeting this intended audience to check if it reacts as we thought.

The second way is to find places where your target audience communicates and to find out the answers to these questions directly from them. That was what I was doing at the beginning of my career when I didn't have any clients. We will analyze this method further in more detail.

What do you actually sell?

I really want you to understand what exactly you are selling. It is clear that people buy your product or service. But this makes a little more sense. People don`t buy the product or service itself; they buy a solution to certain problems and tasks in the form of your product, they buy emotions and satisfaction of their needs.

Throughout the last 4 years, I have been falling the victim of one very exquisite manipulation. Well, if I made this mistake once, I would be okay with that, but it happens every year. I'm talking about the purchase of a gym membership.

My last purchase of the gym membership took place last year and it was super-intelligent. During the last year, I attended the gym exactly 5 times. As a result, one training cost me $35. Remember how fitness clubs sell themselves? What do they say in advertising? What is written in advertising texts? What is shown in the videos?

Here is what their advertising messages are all about: «Be beautiful, athletic and healthy», «Be a slim beauty and have the world on a string». In fact, you are being sold the result that you can get!

I can guarantee that you have not seen an advertisement where you would be told: « Hey man, do you want to go to the gym? Attend the gym 3 times a week, preferably from 7 am, in order to be in time for your work, and exercise for 2 hours. And switch to advanced level, sweat like its hell, work out through the muscle pain – as it is the only way you'll get your muscles to grow. Most likely, you will not return after the first training. But if you still come, you will get to hate your coach after it. Therefore, only today we offer an annual membership for just 200$. If you want to come with your wife, we have a special offer for couples for just 250$ »

And here is an alternative text for ladies:

«The gym is waiting for you to come 5 times a week, where you will be engaged in sweaty workouts to lose 2pounds, but this will not help if you continue to eat wrong foods. Therefore, aside from the workouts, you will have to stop eating bread, sweets, fats, alcohol and eat after 18:00 too, you will need to go to bed before 22:00, because if you do not fall asleep before that time, you will want to eat. And it is absolutely forbidden! All this pleasure will cost you only 200$ annually»

Nobody sells like that. Everyone omits these moments. Sell what they want to buy. In this case, this is the result that the client dreams of.

Let`s talk about how to sell cosmetics or perfumes. You have seen such an advertisement on TV. In the centre of attention, there is a very beautiful girl, as a rule, or a movie star, and all the guys are going crazy about her. And the meaning of the advertising is - buy perfume and all the guys will be yours. Buy cosmetics and be irresistible!

Or for example, courses and training. We sell the result, the emotions that a person will receive after signing up for it. That is happiness. And so, we regularly buy, because we want to get the result and be happy.

By the way, while writing these lines! I received a text message on the phone with the following text: «Get a discount over 90% for the gym membership until August 31. Hurry up to buy the maximum package at a super price of $110 »

What would you advise me to do? At the end of the chapter, I will write what I have decided.

Have you seen the advertisements for exercising equipment? I used to love watching the ads featuring a pumped-up man and a very beautiful girl advertising a home exercising unit. Just by looking at this duo, people get the impression that they got these dream bodies thanks to this unit only. If you ever bought a fitness machine, you will agree with me.

As soon as I bought this home exercising unit, I was waiting for it as a child waits for Santa Claus. I was full of expectations. I was already almost seeing my perfect abs in the mirror. Okay, they were covered by my belly, but I perfectly saw how I would look like the guy from the advertisement.

And then it arrived. I immediately began exercising every day for 45 minutes. And this is 2 times more than necessary. I just needed these abs now, not in a month.

I kept exercising for a week, then the second, but my enthusiasm was fading. Then I went for 15 minutes of exercising, just like it was mentioned in advertising. And then I just forgot about it. And this exercising unit became just a garment hanger or used otherwise, but nothing like the means of reaching the perfect shape. But at the time of purchase, I sure did not think so.

We are confident that we would be exercising, just because we see such texts and promises in the advertising – exercise for just 15 minutes a day and you will get the desired abs, while all the girls will look like models.

Another example:

Why do we go to the dentist? As a rule, we want to get rid of the pain. This is the most common reason. And if the doctor helps us, then we will be happy to pay for it. The stronger the pain, the faster we want to get rid of it. The bigger our problem is, the faster we want to solve it. That is why we need to know the pain and the problems of our customers.

Pain points and problems of customers

When I was launching my first training for advertising on Google, I had no students yet. But there was another positive point. I was in my students' shoes, I knew very well what pains my customers had, what problems arise throughout the work process, or in the family, what people want from life, what people want to spend money on, how much they want to earn. In addition, I did one very simple thing. I found 5 forums where my target audience communicates and spied on what they were writing there about things important to them.

And I came across one very interesting competitor site, where people were asked 2 very simple questions: «What do you want to get thanks to this profession? » and «What are you dreaming about? »

Under these questions, there were more than 300 answers, where people really shared their dreams. And you know, I was very surprised when 80% of 300 people wrote that they wanted to travel, help their parents and the most powerful moment: «stop working for food». It turned out that people had a huge problem; they, working for someone, could not earn decent money and were tied to the office, to the employer.

Everything that I learned from my target audience on this site I used in advertising and on my own site. Now imagine when I used the phrase «you want to travel », «help parents», «stop working for food», I began to simply read the minds of my clients, and in my advertising texts they easily recognized themselves. With the thoughts shaped up in the desired way, they were clicking the link in my advertisement and signing up for the training.

Therefore, if you still do not know your target audience, find forums or sites where your target audience communicates and see what they write, what problems they have, what they dream about. All this will greatly help you create the offer that they cannot refuse.

You will be reading the minds of your clients, like Mel Gibson did in the «What Women Want»

I hope you remember how easily he managed to make women fall in love with him. And this is not weird, because he knew exactly what they wanted. He could easily find an approach to any woman. And they all wanted different things.

Right in the next subchapter, we will talk about how to properly divide the target audience to give it exactly what it wants.

Customer portrait

How do I understand that I have a portrait of a client? Well, it's when I can imagine my client physically. In order to create a portrait of the client, you have to answer a number of questions. Think up the name of your client, determine their gender, age, passion, income, marital status, number of children, profession, think about what they can do during their off-hours, what problem of this client might be solved by using your product or service, why they should choose you, what they dream of. Describe one of your clients in great detail.

For myself, I wrote the story of my client, relying on the points written above.

It looks like this:

Hello, my name is Serge. I am 31 years old; I am married and I have a daughter. I work in a bank. I earn 200$ per month. I also combine the main job with some work on the Internet. It all started with the search for online income. After I've checked a lot of information, I opted for selling from websites. At first, I wanted to open an online store, but then I went for a landing page, but I was facing the problem of contextual advertising.

I started reading, watching online courses and I realized that this is an interesting profession that makes me constantly learn something new. Frankly speaking, then there was a choice between advertising and programming. For now, I chose the advertising path. Maybe one day I will start learning to programme too. I decided to get engaged in sales on the internet and learn to contextual advertising, then social networks.

The reason for that is I don't need a lot of money to start. The ultimate goal is to sort out several niches, find a good niche and build an effective sales funnel.

This is how I do it, in this format, it's easier for me to remember. So, when I need to write an advertisement, I always have client stories on my mind. And I write my texts for them.

Analyzing Competitors

My sister and her husband decided to get into selling women's clothes and asked me to help them sell on Instagram. I agreed and began working. They were dealing with the selection of goods for sale and photos. My task was to promote their business on Instagram and Facebook.

We signed up for an Instagram account, added photos of the products, made a description of them. We had beautiful photos from photo shoots (they were provided by the manufacturer) on beautiful models.

Thus we launched the first advertisement.

We started receiving messages from potential customers. Someone asked about the price, size, delivery. But they didn't buy. So, the first month passed. The Instagram audience has reached 10,000 people. Everyone continued to be interested in the product, but no one was buying it. We realized that the audience that is interested in the product is not how I imagined. The more the merrier. We restarted the advertisement to the right audience and there were even more appeals. We even sold 2 dresses. But it was not what we dreamed about! At some point, I even surrendered to despair as I could not understand where the problem was. What were we doing wrong?! And then we stumbled upon competitors. They were selling exactly the same product, with the same photos, but 1,5 - 2 times cheaper. And then another, and another competitor.

All of them were selling cheaper. And then everything became clear. We and all competitors have been like the two drops of water similar to each other. No uniqueness, no difference. And then the price factor came first, and we lost this battle.

I was sure that I did not need to do an analysis of competitors because I have my experience. I was so wrong! And I've lost time and money! good experience received, but it is a pity that it cost me so dearly!

I am sure that you are familiar with such a concept as a unique trading offer. The point is to be different from competitors, to have an advantage that competitors do not have, and a more advantageous offer than competitors.

And for this, we need to analyze them. This will give us the opportunity to understand what they are already offering, how they offer, where they offer, to whom they offer.

The best difference from competitors that we can find is your personality. Yes, of course, the difference may also be in your offer for your clients: you can offer more for less money, offer various additional options and interesting terms of purchase.

But your personal brand, if you would be promoting it, will make it so that you can earn more. And there will be no need to fight with customers for the price. People will buy from you because you are selling or creating it.

It happens that it is difficult to identify competitors. And many of our students say that they have no competitors. I can tell you that if you have no competitors, this is not very good. But often everyone has competitors and a lot of them.

Who are the competitors? These are the companies where your target audience leaves their money.

View your competitors' Facebook and Instagram accounts. How many followers do they have? How are their accounts shaped up? What do your competitors write about? Which of the posts are most liked? And comments? What giveaways do they run? What promotions and discounts do they give?

Segmentation of your target audience

In this paragraph, I will explain to you a new concept, such as segmentation of your target audience.

Segmentation of the target audience is the division of the audience into groups that unite people on the basis of similar needs (requests).

Wikipedia indicates that segmentation of TA is «a crucially important aspect of marketing». And it is true. Segmentation of the target audience and the market is important for the promotion on the Internet and social networks.

The tools that are used for segmentation, divide the audience into groups and allow you to send the most appropriate advertising message to each individual group, depending on the preferences of users, rather than the advertiser's internal perceptions. With equal advertising costs, the effectiveness of a segmented campaign will be higher.

How will customer segmentation allow you to run away from competitors?

First of all, you are building your ad campaign better than the competitors, because their audience is not segmented. While your competitors will try to stab in the dark, you will sell the goods to the right customer with the help of the right texts.

Secondly, you will formulate the offers and benefits that your customers need.

How can you carry out the segmentation correctly? Let's look at a simple example: «How to set up advertising on Facebook? »

Imagine that you offer to teach the people how to set up advertising on Facebook. You go to Facebook, make a post saying you can teach people to set up ads. And it seems to be a clear, good offer, but let us improve it.

In this case, we understand that the target audience is entrepreneurs. But entrepreneurs can be very different. Therefore, our next task is to break the target audience of entrepreneurs into 4 segments: there is a large business segment, small business segment, online business segment, and offline business segment. This is a rather rough segmentation as if you delve, for instance, into the small business, it can be further divided into restaurant owners, psychologists, beauty salons, travel agencies, etc. I think you have caught the gist.

Now our offer may look differently: «How can a psychologist learn how to set up advertising on Facebook and get two times more clients?», «How can a travel agency increase its profit by 2 times through Facebook advertising?», «How can a restaurant owner increase the number of visitors by promoting on Facebook», «How to organize a flow of clients to a beauty salon through Facebook advertising».

As you can see, all these offers now have a specific audience. The payout from this advertising with such an offer will be several times higher. In this example, we have segmented the audience by its sphere of activity.

How else can you segment your audience? By geo-location. Choose a country of residence, city, district, region, street.

We can apply this segmentation principle when we advertise goods across Ukraine. As you know, in Ukraine, part of the population speaks Russian and others – Ukrainian only. By segmenting the audience by region, we can compile an ad in Ukrainian for Western Ukraine, thereby obtaining more advertising payouts. And for the eastern part, we can make an advertisement in Russian, thereby also increasing the benefits of the advertising.

The does re is another way of segmentation. It`s according to social economic characteristics. These characteristics include education, income, and solvency of the audience.

I often hear such a question from my clients: «How can I find a solvent audience? After all, everyone wants to sell to people who have money. »

And it really is very easy to do with Facebook ads. It so happened that there are luxury products that not all people can afford. For example, a few people have an iPhone 10 or 8+, and there are even those who do not use Apple technology at all. Therefore, by choosing an audience in the advertising settings based on the presence of «apple» technology, it is more likely that this audience has money. Though it's not a universal truth.

Another segmentation option is demographic. It includes the age of the client, gender, marital status. This feature has a very strong impact on customers. For example, adolescents and students are very prone to emotional low-cost purchases, while older people tend to think about a decision more and compare more.

Very often in our advertising campaigns, we limit the age of people. Without this setting on, we would never launch the advertising, just because people of different ages make decisions in different ways. The way I made decisions at age 25 is very different from my own decision-making at 33.

Women make decisions in their own way, more emotionally. Men - on the contrary - adhere to logic. Therefore, segmentation of the audience, even into men and women, will be a big advantage for your advertising campaign.

For example, we went for that segmentation when promoting a cleaning company with «apartment cleaning» services. We divided the audience into women and men. We showed the women a picture in advertising, which depicted a few very sad ladies with a rag in their hands. And the text in the picture was like: «Again, spending all the weekend on cleaning? Enough! Call us - we will do all the household chores for you». And below they described the corresponding chores: wash the windows, remove the dust in the most inaccessible places ».

At the same time, there was another picture for men: a man watching a football match, with a text «Watch football, we will do everything for you». In the case of men, there are completely different benefits: it is not so important for a man to wash windows or remove dust in hard-to-reach places. The main thing for them is the specifics: we will do it in 3 hours and it costs 20 dollars.

Additional methods of segmenting your audience include interests, for example. After all, there are girls who are interested in sports, handmade, cooking, business, raising children? And all these girls can be addressed in different ways.

How else can you get information about your target audience? Of course, by communicating with them. Ideally, you can use a questionnaire, which will give you the information you need about your customers.

You can create a questionnaire with four to five questions that are important to you. And ask your customers to complete this form for you. Yes, perhaps most of them will not fill it, but even these 10–15% of people who will fill out your questionnaire will help you understand the audience even better. Conduct surveys asking about the values of your target audience.

Advertising texts. Trying Offers. Offers which you cannot refuse.

To begin with, let's see what advertising on Facebook and Instagram consist of: a picture or video, title, and text of the ads. In different formats, the ad can be modified, but these three basic elements are always present.

Let's analyze each element of the advertisement and find out what it is responsible for.

Picture/video/slideshow is the most significant element in an advertisement, as namely, it is responsible for attracting attention.

Remember how you check your feed on Facebook or Instagram.

Check it right now on your phone. You do it quickly by swiping your thumb across the screen. The feed rapidly runs up, but at some point, you stop. You stop only because your attention was attracted by a picture or video, and you were interested to see what was there.

I think I don't need to say that if your ad has a non-catching picture or video, it will be flipped through and no one will pay attention to it. And our goal is different. We want to make sure that as many people as possible pay attention to our advertising.

The next element is the title. It is a significant element in the advertisement. It stands out in bold capital letters and is responsible for the interest. The purpose of the title is very simple. It should encourage a potential client to read the first sentence of the text. With the headline, we need to sell the person the desire to read the rest of the text. I will give you some header cliché that I regularly use.

The first cliché: Announce the biggest benefit!
Describe what the customer will receive:
«How to increase the income of a travel agency by 2 times in just 1 month? »

«How to get the body of a Greek God in just 3 months of individual workouts with a coach? »

«How to learn to sing in just 3 lessons in our vocal school? »

The second cliché: Remind about the biggest problem.

The purpose of this title is to unleash a person's desire to solve a problem more quickly:

«How to shed off the extra 10 pounds in just a month without training and diets? »

«How to get more customers in your business thanks to the targeted advertising on Facebook? »

«How to get rid of baldness in just 3 procedures in our centre? »

The third cliché: Intrigue.

The purpose of this title is to create intrigue so that people would like to read the rest of the post and learn something like:

«How can a mother of an infant sleep soundly at night? »

«Do you like to eat at night?" Learn how to do it without gaining extra pounds! »

«How to continue to smoke safely? »

The fourth cliché: Create a sensation. Such headlines are often used by newspapers.

The purpose of this title again is to arouse the interest in reading the rest of the text. How do we usually react to some kind of sensation? We are interested to know what is really there. The sensation is very easy to create.

Start your ads with the words «finally» followed by any kind of text. You can try:

«Finally, we found the possibility to look 10 years younger».

«Only for girls. We finally made it. Look ... »

«How long have we been waiting for this! And today you have the unique opportunity to enrol in our course. »

The fifth cliché: Make an offer that cannot be refused.

Consider how you can offer your goods and services so that if a person decides to refuse, they will feel that they are losing something important. Make sure that the client has no doubts.

For example:

«We will deliver pizza in 30 minutes. If we are late, we won't ask for payment».

In 2 months, you will learn to speak English fluently or we will refund you 150% of the course fee.

«You double your income as part of our training. Or we will refund your money».

I'll give you a list of words which you can start the headline with:

How.

Who else wants to?

Attention!

Finally.

Find out how!?

What if you? (I like to start texts with this phrase so much. This phrase allows you to draw a picture in the human imagination. For example: «What if you lost 10 pounds? How would your life change? »

When a person reads this sentence, they would draw this picture and imagine themselves just like that and even what they would feel at this moment. And then your task in the text is to offer your service/product and prove that this can be easily achieved with you.

The third element of ads is the ad text.

The task of the text is to induce the desire to perform an action. At the end of the text there must be a call to action - what you want your potential client to do: call, write, like, etc.

So, how can you make a person want to know more, order a consultation or purchase your product or service?

Your offer should be profitable. Therefore, as a rule, we fill the ad text with benefits for the client. What will the client gain by agreeing to get your offer? What emotions will they feel? What kind of problem they will solve? Write out 10–20 benefits that your customers will get from purchasing goods or services. Spend as much time as possible on creating your offer. Just one good offer that you would make to your customers may allow you to lift your business to a new level.

Same happened with me. 9 years ago, I began my career in Internet marketing. I started with the development of websites. I was working in many agencies and creating websites. I started from small to large online stores. At that time, I was just designing websites, working in an agency, but I always wanted my own business. Yes, I did not like to depend on salary. Although at that time I was earning some decent money, around 700USD per month. But I decided to quit at the most difficult moment for me: my wife and I were just waiting for our child. She, Irina - that is my spouse's name - was five months pregnant.

I will say right away that even before this I was thinking about working for my own.

I was rather tired of working for someone. Even probably not as tired as I understood that: first, I needed more free time (so that I would not have to constantly ask for permission to leave because I had to help my wife); secondly, of course, it was a question of money. I was sure that I could earn more without working in the office. And made the appropriate decision.

Before leaving, I found several projects for the first month to earn money. Thus, one month has passed. I'll say right away that in the first month I made only two sites and earned $ 1,400 – the equivalent of my salary for 2 months in the agency.

But it was too early to rejoice since there were no new projects. I knew a few people. I needed to make myself known on the market. And without any advertising, it is very difficult to start your own business.

I got engaged in advertising even when I was still employed in the web-design agency. My first advertising was the one I made for my spouse – she is a child psychologist. The second advertising I did for my own services.

To be honest, it was a very difficult period, and I had to spend a lot of money on advertising. It was very sad, because, in the niche of website development, the price per click already reached $ 10-15, and now, it is probably even more. At that moment I almost stopped believing in all these advertisements and sites.

But I knew for sure that I would not return to work, because of this too awesome feeling of doing something for yourself and your future. Thus, you understand why you get up early in the morning. Moreover, at that moment I already had my daughter, Masha.

Then I tried a lot of different options for advertising myself and ways to find people who would need my service. At one point, people began to contact me through advertising. I got the first customers. But for this I had to do everything differently: direct advertising did not work. People did not understand that I could make them a quality website and advertising. And I decided to carry out free consultations on how to create websites, and it was only in this way that I was able to find clients.

I analyzed my competitors and was trying to find things I could use as my advantages. And I managed to find this uniqueness that no one in the market had. I began to offer people to set up advertising, and as a gift, I made a website. The selling site, known as the Landing page.

I launched the advertising on social networks with this offer - «Order an advertising campaign setup - get a website as a gift», and in the first month I received over 200 applications, and over the next six months, I created about 100 advertising campaigns and websites. Then I worked without even re-launching the advertising. There were lots of orders. I polished the skills of setting up advertising to such a level that all the projects I took brought wonderful results for my clients.

I worked for the result. And this was what became the decisive factor. And that was what distinguished me from all the other specialists.

For example, we agreed with the client that I would set up the advertising. I did it, but there was no result. Then I re-designed the client`s site and brought it to good sales levels. I did not charge for the design of the site. And customers couldn't help but like that. Moreover, they were delighted. And they began to recommend me to other entrepreneurs.

Think about how you can make an offer for your clients and what result you can give them so that they would want to recommend you.

So, you already have almost everything to launch a successful advertising campaign.

I suggest you do this. And then we will deal with how to optimize advertising, how to test it in such a way to spend less, but receive more applications from potential customers.

How to avoid spending money in vain?

The most frequently asked question by newbie advertisers is: «How to not spend money on advertising and get nothing? »

I recommend starting an advertising campaign with the audience that knows you. With your warm audience.

Therefore, first of all, you need to start advertising targeting your customers with an offer to purchase your other products or services.

Or run ads targeting people who have already interacted with your content on a business page on Facebook or Instagram. Or people who watched your videos. Or people who visited your site.

Running the Advertising campaign

So, we are smoothly moving to run an advertising campaign. What does it mean to run an advertising campaign?

After you have launched your advertising campaign and it started working, you will receive the first statistics. This means that you can now see how much one click on your ad is worth or how much engagement in your advertising post (likes, comments, clicks on the link) is costing you, and how much you have spent on getting leads.

An advertising campaign is like a one-year-old child who has just started walking. And they strive to go somewhere constantly. You have to constantly keep an eye on them: so that they do not fall, do not run out onto the road, do not catch on other children and avoid getting knocked down. And you need to explain to them what can be done and what is forbidden. For example, touching the socket and eating from the floor is totally prohibited.

So, running the advertising campaign implies that the advertising campaign must be monitored. And when you receive the first statistics, you need to decide which advertising is not working (or is expensive) and needs to be turned off, and which one worked well and can be further polished and used.

Next, we will consider the statistics. How to test your advertising and how to spend less money and attract more customers?

How to spend less on advertising and attract more customers? Advertising optimization

On the advertising account, there are several basic indicators. Let's take a look which of them you need to pay attention to when launching an advertising campaign.

Coverage. This is the number of people who have seen your ad at least once.

Impressions. This is the total number of times your ad is shown to people. This indicator can be higher than the coverage since your Facebook and can be seen by one person several times.

Result. The average price for the result after viewing the advertisement. The price for the result shows how much money you spend on achieving the objectives of the advertising campaign. Thus, you can see how well your ads work. The higher price means fewer people respond to your ads. With this indicator, you can compare the performance of different campaigns and identify the opportunities for obtaining the best results. It helps you understand which rate to select for future ad groups.

Budget. This is the maximum amount you want to spend on an advertising campaign.

The amount spent. This is the total amount you have already spent on your ad campaign.

Evaluation of relevance. The score from 1 to 10 determines how well the target audience responds to advertising. This figure appears as soon as more than 500 ad impressions are completed.

This is exactly the indicator that I want you to focus on. Depending on this evaluation, you will be able to understand how well your audience responds to advertising. If the evaluation of relevance equals 1 - this means that your advertising is not relevant, and the audience is not interested in it. When it is at 10, it means the advertising is at the peak of relevance. Based on the number of impressions, Facebook gives you the score. Therefore, the higher it is - the better the result you will get. A good value is from 7 to 10.

How to analyze the results of an advertising campaign?

This section has a lot of numbers. I know people who just love statistics and analyzing the data.

Honestly, I like statistics, but I'm not an ardent fan of it. Due to my profession, I need to understand how it works. But for the majority, it is difficult and not interesting. Therefore, let us analyze the statistics using the «Food» subject that is easy to understand for everyone.

You all attended parties throughout your life or organized them yourself in cafes or restaurants. And you had to order the dishes from the menu. Just imagine such a situation. You have made an order. It includes 3 Caesar salads, 3 Olivier salads and 3 salads with shrimps. And so it happened that all the guests ate the «Caesar» and didn`t touch the «Olivier», and the guests ate only one salad with the shrimp.

Here it is, our statistics! You analyzed and concluded that next time you will be most likely ordering more Caesar salads, as it is popular, while you won't be ordering Olivier salad at all, and order just one serving of shrimp salad.

Thus, the guests will be satisfied, because they will not be leaving hungry, and this will even save your money.

Now let's find out how we can save the advertising budget using the advertising campaign statistics we obtained. What opportunities do we have in this case?

The «Age» Indicator. You can look at the age of people who filled the applications or responded to your advertising posts. And what age group was not interested in your offer at all.

And if you find that people between the ages of 35 and 44 are the most active audience, then why not show even more advertisements to this particular audience. And, for example, turn off the impressions for the 45+ age group, as it is not effective.

The «Gender» indicator. You can find out who responds better to your advertisements: men or women. And if it turns out that men practically do not fill your applications, then you can turn off the display of adverts to them. Thereby saving the budget.

The «Age and Gender» indicator. You can look at both age and gender at the same time and find out which audience responds better to advertising.

The Country indicator. If you start advertising in several countries, you can use this indicator to determine in which country you have a better return on advertising. And again, disable ads in inefficient countries.

The «Region» indicator. If you launch your campaign in several regions, you can also see which region responds better to advertising.

The «Device» indicator. You will see the statistics of the devices from which people respond to your advertising. It can be a personal computer, iPhone, Android smartphone, Android tablet or iPad. These statistics will give you an understanding of what your audience is using.

I had a lot of cases when advertising worked very well on the users of personal computers and very bad on mobile phone users. Then I just turned off the display of ads for mobile devices.

The «Platform» indicator. You can find out where people respond best to your advertisements on Facebook, Instagram or Messenger.

The «Placement» indicator. It helps determine which ad space is as effective as possible for you. The point is to divide advertising by placement. Facebook Feed and Instagram Feed have different picture formats. That is why one ad group should be made for Facebook and shown only on Facebook and the second group of ads only on Instagram.

The «Time of the day» indicator allows you to determine at what time people respond best to your ads. The breakdown, in this case, is hourly. For example: from 1 pm to 2 pm or from 4 pm to 6 pm.

In this way, you will find out the best time to place your advertisements, and later on, in the ad display settings, you can specify the correct time to start the advertising.

A/B testing

A / B testing or Split testing allows you to test various advertising options and select the most effective ones. It is carried out in order to improve the results of future campaigns.

Let's make it even easier. When we analyzed our target audience and decided to make a definite offer to this audience, we assumed that exactly this offer will be interesting for this audience. Before we launched the advertising and got a real result, this would be just an assumption.

That is why we need to conduct a series of tests in order to understand whether our assumption was really successful or something needs to be changed. You should understand that until the test has been launched, no one would ever tell you what result you would get. Anything that is not tested in actual practice will be an assumption or, in another way, a hypothesis.

Very often I come across a situation when advertising works fine in one region, and in another region, it is far not as good as we would like it to be. And there is always an explanation why this is so.

I have a client who is engaged in training massage therapists. He teaches people a new profession of «massage therapist». His school has branches in four cities: Odessa, Lviv, Kharkov, and Kiev.

We launched the first advertisement in Odessa - and got an excellent result. We easily gathered a group for a course of massage therapists. Further, we launched the same advertising campaign in Lviv, and also got a great result. The last was Kharkov, and the same advertising campaign did not work at all there. The same site, the same texts, the same settings of the advertising campaign did not produce any results. We could not understand what was the problem until we started asking people why they weren't getting enrolled in the course in Kharkov.

As it turned out, there was a competitor in Kharkov, which has been on the market for a long time, and the cost of their courses was two times higher than ours. And all the people signed up for that course, although we had very good specialists, and a wonderful course, the price was two times lower and people decided that if we had such a low price, then the course should have been not so effective. We did not expect such an answer. Therefore, think 10 times before setting a low price. Perhaps you will have the same situation.

This is a story to ensure that everything needs to be tested. I just want to say that Facebook carries out a lot of tests for you. For example, you created the advertising with the objective of «lead generation» across Ukraine, targeting an audience with an age ranging from 18 to 65 years, both men and women who have business interests then chose all possible types of placement and created 3 different ads.

And after this, you have launched the advertising. What happens next? Facebook starts showing your ads to all of this audience, but after a while, it notices that a certain audience responds to the ad and leaves requests. It finds out that men aged 35–44 years from Kiev who are using their iPhone mobile phones and Facebook feed leave more applications than all the other groups. And the price of these applications is much lower than that of the other audiences.

Facebook has an algorithm that tries to optimize your advertising as much as possible - it starts to show less of the adverts to other audience and only covers the one that leaves the applications. In fact, Facebook independently conducts A

/ B testing for you, determining the most effective promotion channel.

But there is one small cave. Imagine that these men who leave the applications do not buy anything, then it turns out that you spent money on advertising, you received the applications, but there is no profit and no sales. Facebook does not know about this and continues to show your ads exclusively to this audience, and the audience that could have bought your products sees your ads less and less frequently.

It turns out that Facebook is doing us a good deed, trying to help, but the result is the opposite.

Therefore, now we will talk about how to segment and scale an advertising campaign correctly.

What might and should be tested first:

First of all, we need to test the «ad format». It's your pictures, videos, slideshows. In each ad group, we should create 6 ad formats. We can write one advertising text and select 6 different pictures/videos for it.

The purpose of this test is to determine the best picture/video for advertising.

After we have determined the best advertising formats, we can test advertising texts. You should write several advertising texts, but now with one and the same picture/video.

Thus, we can understand which text is the most effective.

What else can you test?

Audience

According to the region. You can run the same advertising in different regions and thus determine which region it works better and more efficiently.

According to age. You can run your ads targeting different age groups and thereby determine what age group responds best to your ads and places the orders.

According to gender. You can test the reactions of men and women.

According to the interests. You can test the behaviour of people with different interests.

Placement

You can also test different placements. For example, Facebook and Instagram feed. Facebook has a built-in split test that it offers you to carry out. Be sure to try.

TIP!

Test only one element at a time. It can be either just a heading, or just a picture, or just some sort of placement, or just gender. If you try to test everything at once, then most likely you will not understand the results of this test. In my practice, there was a case when I first learned what should be tested. I really liked this idea. And since then I taught myself to try everything in practice right away, I immediately launched an A / B test for advertising.

At that time, I was doing advertising campaigns for my website development services. I launched 2 ads to check which one works better. And these were completely different ads. And, naturally, one of them turned out to be better and won the competition from the other. And that's all, I kind of conducted the A / B test. What to do next? Create a new ad again? How to understand why one ad was better than another? Was it the title? Picture? Offer? Unfortunately, I wasn't able to figure that out. Therefore, it is very important to test one element at a time.

Reasons your advertising account may get blocked

This happens quite often that Facebook rejects your ads. Let's look at all the possible reasons to prevent this issue.

1. When you first start an advertising campaign, immediately after creating an ad, Facebook asks you to specify the method of payment for the ads. If you choose to pay using your card, then your name on the card should match the name of your Facebook account. If the name differs by at least 1 character, this could be the reason for blocking the advertising account, because Facebook will think that you want to use another person's card.

2. From the latter, it turns out that other people's cards cannot be used in your advertising account. Therefore, if you decide to link a card to your advertising account, then it should be your card

only, and not your brother's, sister's, husband's or wife.

3. Advertising prohibited content:

The first thing you should do before creating an ad is to look at Facebook advertising rules here: https://www.facebook.com/policies/ads.

First, even if you promote an approved product, you can violate Facebook's rules due to the "wrong" ad text.

Secondly, if you have launched an advertisement with prohibited material, and it might have been automatically moderated and launched, then your account will soon be deactivated without the possibility of recovery.

4. People may complain about your ad. And this can cause rejection.

5. Mismatch of the landing page with texts in your ad. Make sure that your ad text is really related to the expectations of the people from your website.

6. You logged in your account from another country. I had exactly that reason for blocking. I sometimes use a VPN that changes my location in the browser. So, Facebook decided that my account was hacked and blocked my advertising account.

7. Your text got too personal, and you are offending people's feelings with it. This is a very frequent reason for rejecting your campaign.

Everything is simple here. As soon as you have created an advertisement, it should be moderated by Facebook before the launch. During this process, the robot checks the content of your text. And if you have a single word which is in the list of prohibited words, the whole text would be rejected. My last case of rejection was due to the word "losing weight". Yes, I understand that this is a very strange reason. But I replaced this word, and the advertisement went through moderation just fine.

There are many more reasons. For example, the one that Facebook simply had an error. Yes, this is also possible.

What needs to be done if this happens?

Facebook can block your advertising account, or only the «payment part», or only the advertisement itself.

Advertisement blocking. In this case, everything is simple, just change the text and send it again to go through moderation.

If the advertising cabinet or «Payments» section is blocked, you need to write to the support service at facebook.com/support, describing the situation and waiting for the moderators' team response.

It may take from 2 to 14 days. You can write many times. But the main thing is to keep writing! And you will be heard. Once they did not respond to my messages for a very long time. And when I finally got the answer, they said that they could not do anything and my account would remain blocked. In this case, you can contact support through their Messenger and chat. In chat, support agents only speak English. Well, at least I came across only English-speakers. If you do not know English well, then use the Google translator. It will help you!

Here is a practical task

- Determine an advertising objective.
- Define your target audience.
- Find out the interests of the target audience.
- Determine the placements: where you are planning to run the advertising.
- Determine your advertising budget.
- Choose the ad format.
- Write a headline for your advertisement.
- Write the text.
- Choose a picture / video / slideshow to advertise.
- Run and test an ad campaign.
- Analyze your advertising campaign.

- Increase the budget for that advertisement that gave the best results.

AFTERWORD

Alex AL-VATAR

I can feel, by the end of this book, you might think «Oh, gods, there is so much information, so many tools, and opportunities, so much to be learned. How will I break down all this information in my head? »

So, I will try to simplify everything for you. Most likely, apart from our book, our master classes, and pieces of training, you are watching and listening to other experts. Everyone has their own opinion. You got some knowledge and you became confused. It happens.

You know, I`ll give you a magic pill right now!

Maybe you remember, in our childhood, we were told by our parents or maybe today you are telling this to your children: «Well if we had a money-making machine, we would be living differently». Is it familiar to you? Our parents were saying the same thing and it sounded like magic.

But I grew up, became independent, and today I am deeply convinced that each of us has such a money-making machine. It's in our head. Each of us can figure out a way to earn money. Many people simply don`t understand how to do this. So, I will help you understand how to make money on social networks, attracting customers and selling your products and services.

Imagine that there is a money-making machine and it has only 3 buttons. These are the 3 tools with the help of which you will find your client, make a sale and earn money. It is due to the fact that, no matter how many tools in Internet marketing you have seen, all of them can be divided into 3 types:

1. Coverage tools

This includes all the tools and ways to show your message to people. These are Facebook and Instagram targeting, publications and reposts, Google ads, bulletin boards, and other sites. How to understand that this is a « coverage tool»? In these services and programs, you pay for impressions, for making people see your message.

2. Capture tools

This includes all the tools which we can use to get the contacts of potential customers. These are the lead forms, websites, personal pages, business pages, phone numbers, e-mail address, and so on.

The purpose of using these tools is to get an opportunity to contact the client. Get in touch with them.

3. Communication tools

This includes all the tools with the help of which we can communicate with people: calls, e-mails, messages in Messenger, chatbots, mailing lists.

Thus, overall, no matter what they say at the workshops and in the books, in order to attract a client, you need to use only 3 tools:

- Coverage.
- Capture.
- Communication.

At the same time, you can use different ways to attract customers. Start experimenting and combining different tools.

For example:

To reach your target audience:
• publish and launch targeted advertising on Facebook.

To get contacts:
• indicate a link to a site in the advertising publication where the client can leave a phone number by filling a certain application.

To communicate with the client:
• Call the client using the phone number left in the application form.

If this method did not work, try combining other tools with each other.

Here is another example:

To reach your target audience:

• make a post on your personal page.

To get contacts:

• In this post, ask those who are interested in your offer to write you a private message.

For communication:

• use the messenger. You can write or call the client directly in the application.

Has it become a little clearer? Great. Now you can invent and create your own ways to sell on the Internet. Remember that money-making machine is in your head.

Now that you have read this book, you have all the necessary tools to attract clients from social networks. You already understand that Facebook and Instagram have different promotion strategies, and you should choose the one that will be the most effective for you.

You already know what content you need to create for running your profile on social networks. We discussed how to create this content. All instructions will stay with you in this book and you can use them in the future.

You know how Instagram works, what are the ways to become more famous and attract customers in this social network. You learned about GiveAways and their types. We prepared a step-by-step action plan for taking part in such events aimed at attracting a new audience.

You got familiar with the features of a Facebook advertising account. So even when you first open the laptop and go to the advertising cabinet, it will be difficult for you to understand what is the purpose of each of the buttons in the interface and how to use the advertising cabinet, but the most important thing you have already got, and this is the clear understanding of your capabilities depending on what you want to get from the advertising. You can figure out how to use the interface of the advertising office in 1 day, by simply watching the video tutorials on YouTube or you can find a marketer and ask them to show and explain you everything.

Well, we shared with you the criteria for the effective management of your advertising campaign. This is what we pay attention to in order to attract more customers from Facebook and Instagram and spend less money on advertising.

All this knowledge is yours now. So just start using the knowledge and methods of promotion described in this book!

Acknowledgements

We want to thank you for reading this book and giving us an opportunity to share our experiences and our thoughts with you. Now, we are sharing the same views with you.

May great success become a part of your journey!

Best wishes,
Alexandr Kalinin, Igor Osetsimskiy, Alex Al-Vatar

About the authors

Many people who achieve any success or gain significant experience based on personal results at some point are willing to start sharing it with the world. That is exactly what happened to the co-authors of this book.

After taking part in numerous training, seminars, conferences, and providing marketing services to hundreds of clients, Igor and Alexandr decided that it was time to share their knowledge and the experience that was accumulated over a considerable period of time with others. In the beginning, the idea was to simply carry out workshops in different cities and places, share novelties and experiences and travel and just have short vacations in these places. After their first master-mind was held and Igor and Alexandr made it so successful, their workshop, named «The flow of customers from Facebook and Instagram» turned into a tour around different cities.

With each new trip, the content was getting refined, improved and something new was added. Sometimes it seemed to be an endless process. Apparently, it was, due to the fact that the attendees asked questions at these events, the speakers had to look for answers and improve their workshop every time.

Later, they decided that they need a third partner who should be able to close down many areas not tackled before, in order to further polish the workshop and course, including the structures, content marketing, video content, etc. This was supposed to be a professional who had repeatedly performed on the stage and had carried out online classes.

Igor and Alexandr needed an initiative partner. Somebody who was as good at marketing as they were.

It was Alex Al-Vatar who became the third partner. They did not discuss how much they would earn from it. They only discussed what they could give to each of those who should have attended their course. Alex very quickly got involved in the process and was making a significant contribution.

The experts wrote down the responsibilities of each other and it worked! Master classes and training have become way more professional.

After they had conducted a sufficiently high number of master classes, marketing training, joint courses, receiving a plethora of positive feedback, they decided to write this particular book – a book where each of them can share the expertise in his field.

Each of the co-authors can write a separate book on marketing. But after the authors have united - this book has become several times more powerful and useful, because it contains twenty years of joint experience in marketing.

The book is written in such a format that everyone can read it: from those who do not have any marketing skills to those who are already engaged in marketing and willing to improve their knowledge or entrepreneurs who feel like they reached a certain level and need a push to make a breakthrough.

Each of the authors is a practitioner, and thus the book includes practical examples, as well as decision-making criteria, in order to deliberately bring some considerable results.

There are a lot of examples from each of the co-authors of the book, so that everyone can apply the knowledge in own experience, find a similar situation in their own business and understand what needs to be done to really get a «customer flow»: what should they do and how should they market their business on the Internet in order to have their sales growing, how to present yourself on the Internet, so that the customers cannot fall behind you.

Thanks to simple actions, great things can be done! So, keep it simple, yet effective!

Igor Osetsimskiy

- Coach and marketing training course speaker.
- Offered 300+ consultations on promotion on Instagram.
- Owner of the Internet marketing agency VerOna.
- The creator of the FlyTOP app – a service to help Instagram accounts get into the top posts.
- Works in internet marketing Since 2011.
- In 2013, he created the first business. During another two years, he has created 5 more businesses. Some of them he successfully sold.
- Provides packaging and promotion services on a monthly basis to 20-30 startup and business owners.
- Used more than $ 50,000 on the advertising budget.
- 200+ businesses are marketed on the Internet by VerOna agency.

Igor has the skills to create, position and run a business on the Internet, and develop a creative promotion strategy. He specializes in promoting a personal brand on Instagram.

Contacts:

Facebook: @Osetsimskiy

Instagram: @Osetsimskiy

VKontakte: @Osetsimskiy

FlyTOP service: https://t.me/FlyTopVerona

Insta-trends: https://t.me/WOWInstaTop

Alex Al-Vatar

- Expert in content for business and project management.
- Coach at content marketing training programs.
- The founder of Flying Markers studio
- Organized more than 100 offline and online master classes for businesses across the CIS.
- Has experience in managing a budget of $ 24,000 for advertising on the Internet.
- Created over 2000 articles, 500 promotional videos, 70 selling websites for businesses.
- In 2016, directed «Maternal Field» movie, which premiered in cinemas in 16 cities across Ukraine.
- Helped the clients sell their goods and services and earn more than $ 500,000 on the Internet.

Author of the «An endless stream of ideas on how to create content for business. »

Contacts:

Facebook: @ alex.alvatar

Instagram: @ alex.alvatar

VKontakte: @ alex.alvatar

Alexandr Kalinin

- Founder of Internet marketing studio « Your Business »
- Official partner of Google in Ukraine
- Author of training programs for marketing and advertising
- Helps entrepreneurs to increase profits with the help of Internet tools and automatic systems for obtaining customers.

Created his first advertising campaign 5 years ago, and since then has created about 250 advertising campaigns for completely different types of businesses with a total advertising budget of more than $500,000.

Throughout his career, he has gained invaluable experience and found all the problematic moments and thousands of reasons why online advertising might not work.

Contacts:

Facebook: @yourbz
Instagram: @kalininpro

For notes

For notes

www.ingramcontent.com/pod-product-compliance
Lightning Source LLC
Chambersburg PA
CBHW060827170526
45158CB00001B/99